FIVE-MINUTE Games

David Pritchard

LONDON
Bell & Hyman

FOREWORD

Most of the games in this book will be new to you. None are trivial and many offer satisfying and varied strategy. In some games no hints are given; this is quite possibly because the games are new or unresearched, so that the best way to play them is not known. If you discover a strategy for any of them, do write and tell us.

Equipment needed is basic, but it is easy to improvise or make your own should this be necessary — sugar lumps, suitably marked with ink, make perfect dice!

Although the majority of the games here are designed for two players, it is usually possible to accommodate more — partnerships can always be formed. Many games too can be adapted for solo entertainment with a little imagination. A one-player game is essentially a puzzle, but almost all the games in this book offer some strategy and looking for this can itself be rewarding. There is something here to challenge every taste. Have fun!

This book was designed and produced by Strawberry Hill Press Ltd,
24 Walpole Road, Twickenham, Middlesex TW2 5SN

First published in 1984 by Bell and Hyman
Denmark House, 37-39 Queen Elizabeth Street, London S.E.1

Design and illustration: Wladek Szechter
Art direction: Richard Souper

ISBN 0 7135 1494 9

Printed in Finland

CONTENTS

3 PEOPLE

GRUBBY OLD MAN

Here's the price of this book in a super little card game, very popular in Sweden, where it originated, but unknown in Britain.

Standard pack, no jokers. Dealer gives three cards face down to each player, the remainder forming the stockpile. The game is in two parts. The first phase is trick-taking. Ace is high and suits are disregarded. Each player puts down one card from his hand face up in turn. The highest-ranking card takes the trick. If two (or all three) players tie – two queens for instance – all three cards are left on the table and the players of the queens play again, highest taking all cards on the table. If again a tie, repeat.

When you play a card you must immediately replace it with one from stock; thus until the end all players have three cards in their hands. The last card in stock is left on the table and belongs to the winner of the last trick. If there is a tie on this, or if any player is without cards, players with cards left in hand add these to their tricks and the player with the lead (i.e., the winner of the previous trick) takes the last card. This is exposed and determines the trump suit in the second phase; thus winner of last trick is assured of at least one trump.

Players now pick up their tricks. These are their hands for phase two when the object is to get rid of all your cards as quickly as possible.

Play is in rotation as usual but now there is an unusual feature: instead of playing a single card a player may at any time play a sequence of cards provided the play is otherwise legal and provided the sequence is all in one suit (example: ◇ J–10–9–8–7).

Phase two starts with the winner of the last trick in phase one leading any card (or cards in sequence). The next player must play a higher-ranking card (or cards) in the suit led. If he cannot do so, he may trump. If he trumps, the third player must go higher in trumps, not in the suit originally led; otherwise third player must beat second player in the suit led. If both second and third players achieve their objectives the table cards are removed from the game and first player leads again. If either second or third player cannot beat the previous player OR IF THEY DON'T WANT TO, then the defaulter must take up into hand all the cards on the table when the lead passes to the next player. Last player in is the Grubby Old Man (a change from Old Maid!).

A typical play in the second phase is illustrated.

Hint

Aim to take about six tricks in the first phase, preferably those with high cards in them.

Phase Two: clubs are trumps

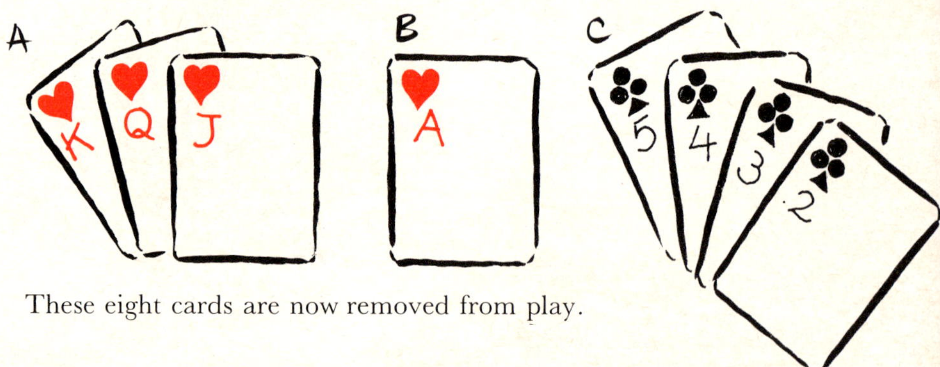

These eight cards are now removed from play.

C is unable, or does not want to beat the ◇J and so picks up the five cards and adds them to his hand. A leads again.

DICE GAME

2 PEOPLE

WIMBLEDON

The best games they say are the simplest and nothing could be simpler than this little tennis game – assuming that you know roughly how to play and score at tennis. You'll need pencil and paper and a couple of dice. An opponent is an asset but not essential.

Draw a straight line on the paper about 10″ long and divide it into twelve parts and number them 0 – 12. They don't have to be measured exactly. Extend line 6 upwards so that your drawing looks like the diagram here.

Marks 0 and 12 are the baselines and 6 is the net. Place a small coin or token on 0. This is the ball. Player A starts by rolling the two dice. If they total 6 or less the serve is into the net, if 7 or more the serve is successful and the coin is placed on the appropriate mark in the opponent's court. A ball in the net allows the player a second service. If it falls short again it is a double-fault and the score is Love – 15. A ball over the net must be returned and player B can elect to throw one or both dice. Player A for his return will have the same option and the rally will continue until one player hits the ball in the net or over the baseline. Score here as in tennis or as in any other similar game (table tennis, badminton for example). It gets a bit tedious after the first set so don't play it too long. Almost no skill (obviously, if the ball falls just your side of the net, you elect to throw one die; if near your baseline you throw them both) but quite a lot of fun. Little girls love it.

Figure 1

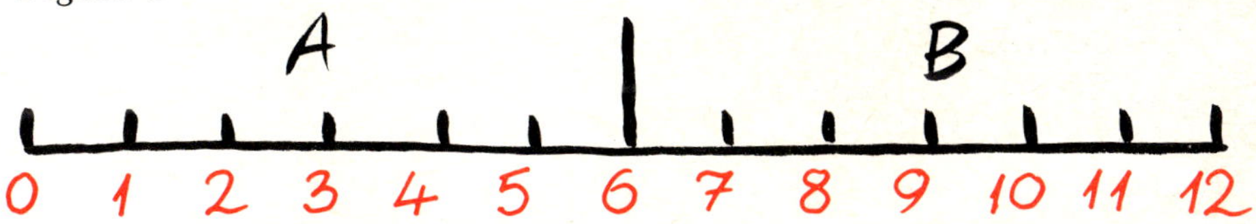

WORD GAME

2 PEOPLE

WORD SQUARES

This is a much abused little game, streets ahead of its reputation. In the first place, there are a variety of accepted scoring systems, most of them suspect. In the second place, the game is usually played in a rather haphazard way with no plan beyond that of completing the word that's just occurred to one.

So shall we start again? Both players draw a 5 × 5 grid on separate sheets of paper which they keep concealed (the grids that is; it's O.K. to let your opponent see your bit of paper provided it's the back).

Each player in turn calls out one letter of his choice. When a letter is announced, BOTH players must enter it in any blank square in their grids before the next letter is called. A letter once entered cannot later be changed or moved.

The object is to form words reading across (left to right) and down, as in a crossword. When 25 letters have been called the grids will be full. Now you score them (you may exchange grids for this purpose if you doubt your opponent's integrity or, more likely, his spelling). It is recommended that you award 10 points for every five-letter word, 5 points for every four-letter word and 3 points for every three-letter word. Two-letter words are not scored and only one word may be scored on any line (you cannot for example score for both SAD and DIG if you happen to have a line SADIG). A completed game is shown in figure 1. A has outplayed B.

So what's profound about it, you ask? The answer is, if you want to take the game seriously, the strategy. Start with the simplest division: you can play offensively, that is to say you play to make the highest possible score, and you do this usually by giving the commonest letters with which it is easy to make words – N, R, S and T plus a few vowels; or you can play defensively with the aim of preventing your opponent from scoring well by giving him some nasty letters like J, Q and Z. Neither of these strategies are satisfactory since they give you no advantage.

The way to play Word Squares intelligently is to start with a strategy but to be prepared to modify or change it as circumstances dictate. Be pragmatic, in other words.

The ideal is to build up a framework of words that you hope your opponent will help you complete – the framework should be flexible so that as many different letters as possible will be acceptable. The whole game is about making use of your opponent's letters and not giving him letters that he will find useful.

So back to strategy. There are many possibilities and there is only room to mention a few here: you will be able to think out some of your own.

Plan to use words that use few vowels (e.g., YACHT) or lots of vowels, or repeat a single letter like F or L. This will embarrass your opponent who will probably be forced, for example, to feed you the vowels you need when all you are doing is giving him consonants he doesn't.

The game is always easy to begin with – no problem about placing say the first half-dozen letters. But you will inevitably reach a stage when you get given letters you positively dislike. So establish a dustbin: a few squares that can least harm your score where you can dispose of unfriendly letters. For this purpose, squares around the middle are usually the best.

There's quite a lot to Word Squares, isn't there?

Figure 1

	10	3	10	5	10
10	C	L	A	M	S
10	H	A	B	I	T
5	I	P	O	L	O
10	D	I	V	E	R
10	E	N	E	M	Y
	A			=	83

	10				10
10	L	E	M	O	N
	A	B	I	P	A
5	R	D	I	M	S
10	C	I	V	E	T
10	H	O	L	E	Y
	B			=	55

A completed game

Hint

Agree beforehand the sort of words that are disallowed – Proper nouns, abbreviations and the like.

PENCIL AND PAPER

2 PEOPLE

LASSOO

Eric Solomon, inventor of Black Box and other well-known games, introduced this sly little time-filler to a gathering of puzzle nuts a short while ago. One suspects that he took a wry pleasure in phrasing the rules.

Lassoo is what is known as a topological game and is in the tradition of Sprouts, facts which further your education but cannot be said to have practical value.

Draw a small grid of dots – say, 4 × 4. You must imagine that at each of these dots there stands a cowboy armed with an unlimited number of lassooes (figure 1).

Taking it in turns to play, you snake out a rope from a cowboy of your choice to lassoo a neighbouring cowboy – i.e., an adjacent dot. The cowboy you noose is known as the lassooee. Of course, you cannot go round doing this indiscriminately because then there would be neither point nor end to the game. Instead, you have to abide by the Sheriff's rules which are:

(1) The lassooer may not be already a lassooee;
(2) The lassooee may not be already a lassooee nor a lassooer; and
(3) No lassoo must cross another lassoo because they'd get entangled.

The winner is the player who makes the last legitimate lassoo. A completed game is shown in figure 2 – no further play is possible.

Hint

If you start, you obviously want the game to end with an odd number of lassooes; if you play second, then you want it to end with an even number. Plan ahead from the beginning to achive your goal. Remember the rule that only a neighbour can be lassooed: that cowboy in the bottom right of figure 2 looks pretty lonely – but that's the way the first player liked it.

Figure 1

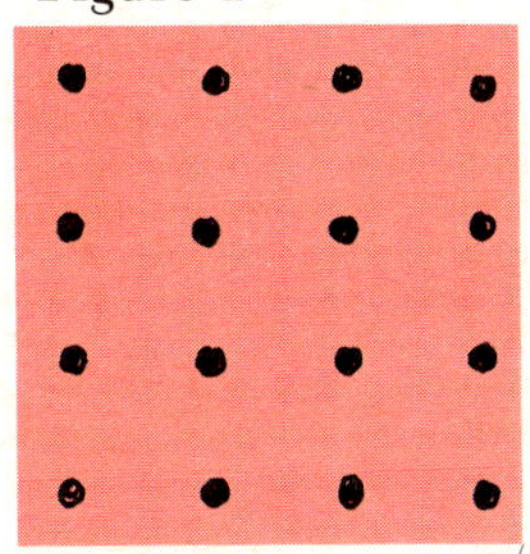

Grid for Lassoo

Figure 2

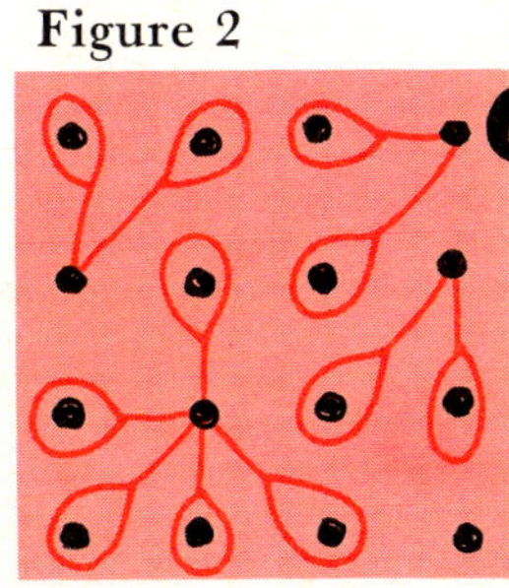

Completed game

WORD GAME

2 PEOPLE

ALPHABET CRICKET

If you are one of those cricket buffs who are perennially baffled by the transparent idiocies of the England selectors, or can recount, in batting order, the side the West Indies fielded against the Australians at Adelaide in '79, then you are certain to be attracted to this basic little cricket game which was invented, it is believed, in the trenches during World War I and has hardly been played since.

The fun (since there is no skill) is in picking a couple of sides that appeal to you (if you are playing solo) or a side to beat that of your opponent if two of you are playing.

First write the two teams down in batting order on a sheet of paper. Now list the letters of the alphabet and against each enter a number, to represent runs, or one of the ways in which you can be out. A typical list is illustrated but no doubt you would prefer to draw up your own.

Now take any book or magazine, open a page at random, and start at the first paragraph (or anywhere else). Suppose you take this piece, starting 'If you are . . .' The first letter is I, which your table tells you scores 2, the second, F, scores 5, and if you go on in this way you will find that your first batsman made a century (125 to be precise) before he was caught. Carry on like this for the rest of the team, ignoring punctuation. That's all there is to it. You can experiment with letter values to make the scoring a bit more realistic.

If you prefer something a little more sophisticated, then this is easily achieved. For example, you could have two letter lists, the second one being for the tail-enders who can be 'out' on one or two of the commoner letters; you introduce this list, say, when the first six wickets have fallen. You can also have fun keeping bowling averages. The side that's fielding nominates a bowler who is naturally changed every over (i.e., after six letters have been called out). There is no limit to the frills you can add!

Scoring Table

A = 1	N = 1
B = 6	O = 3
C = 5	P = caught
D = 6	Q = 25
E = 1	R = 2
F = 5	S = 1
G = 5	T = 1
H = 5	U = 8
I = 2	V = run out
J = stumped	W = 6
K = 10	X = LBW
L = 1	Y = 10
M = bowled	Z = 25

Figure 1

PSYCHOLOGICAL

2 PEOPLE

FOOTSTEPS

This is a subtle little game that exercises both mathematics and mind-reading, particularly mind-reading, which some people are rather good at.

You will find a 'board' useful although the game can be played without one. Take a piece of paper and space out seven marks about an inch apart in a straight line. The central mark can be accentuated though again this is not really necessary. Put a coin or token on the central mark. The board is placed lengthways between the players. (See illustration.)

Each player has an allocation of 50 points. Play is simultaneous: both players write down secretly the number of points they want to spend on the first round and when both are ready they show each other the numbers they have written down.

Higher number is the winner and the player moves the token one mark nearer his opponent. If numbers are equal, nothing happens.

Both players now deduct the number of points they've used from their allocations and then write down the number of points they wish to wager on the second round. Again numbers are compared and the winner moves the token one space nearer his opponent. The first player to get the token on the back mark (that nearest the opponent) is the winner.

Allocations are reduced after each round – the minimum wager permitted is 1 point – and if a player uses up his allocation, then the opponent may continue to play and need only use 1 point per turn to advance the token.

That is all there is to Footsteps although the simple rules hide a lot of strategy. Follow the start of a game in figure 2. There have been six rounds and A is one step into B's territory but he has only 10 points remaining of his allocation whereas B has 28. Short of a miracle, B should win easily.

Hint

The ideal is of course to get just 1 point above your opponent's bid. You might try to convince him that you are planning to play high and then bid 2 on the argument that either he will play high to try and win the round, in which case you will be reducing his remaining point allocation significantly; or he will be throwing it, in which case he is likely to bid the minimum 1 point, in which case you will advance at minimum cost. The trouble with Footsteps is that it is possible to argue the case for almost *any* bid, which is what makes the game fascinating.

You need to be well ahead on points to permit your opponent to advance to the penultimate mark since he will then be in a position to wager ALL his remaining points on the next round – which means that you will have to bid most of yours, just in case. If you play with someone you know well you will find that your respective bids are much closer together than if you play with a casual acquaintance – try it and see!

Figure 1

The 'board'

Figure 2

A game in progress

Bets	Bets
9,4,5,10,3,9	2,4,6,2,7,1

PENCIL AND PAPER

2 PEOPLE

BATTLESHIPS

Battleships is a traditional classroom game that still has a lot of appeal yet most players overlook that it is really a game system rather than a game and so they conscientiously follow the 'rules' that they've learnt from someone else. Yet more than half the fun of the game is in the design, with your imagination the only limiting factor – and it's a lot more rewarding to create your own version of the game than arguing about how many submarines each side should have.

Let's start with the traditional game in case you don't know it. Each player draws two grids on a sheet of paper. The grids can be of any agreed size but 10 × 10 lines is about right for a five-minute game. Both grids are now marked with a notation so that individual squares can be easily identified by name.

On one of these grids, each player enters his fleet by shading in the appropriate number of squares. The ships can be deployed anywhere within the grid, which represents a sea area, but they may not touch one another, not even diagonally. The fleet is made up something like this (everyone has a slightly different version):

1 battleship (4 squares)
2 cruisers (3 squares)
4 destroyers (2 squares)
2 submarines (1 square)

A typical deployment within an annotated grid is shown in figure 1. For example, the cell in which the submarine lower left is located would be referred to as B2.

When both battle fleets have been deployed the next stage begins. Players now take it in turns to fire into each other's sea area with the aim of being the first to sink the enemy's fleet. You can play Battleships using single shots (take it in turns to fire into a single square) or salvoes (usually three shots). This is done by announcing a square or squares thus: 'G4' or 'F3, F4, A1'. The second player refers to his deployment grid and announces any hit(s) thus: 'Hit on cruiser', 'Submarine sunk'. In the event of salvoes, the second player does not announce on which square(s) the hit(s) takes place. The first player now records his shots on his second grid. It is necessary to hit every square of a ship in order to sink it. Figure 2 shows the recording grid used by a player in a single-shot game against the deployment shown in figure 1.

There's very little skill in the game. You naturally want to 'hide' your fleet as best you can but off-beat deployment can be self-defeating in the full meaning of the word: if you put your ships round the edges or group them all down in one corner, your opponent will soon discover this when devastation will follow.

The battleship and cruisers are usually fairly easy to locate but submarines are harder: the first player to sink both of his opponent's submarines usually ends up the winner.

But then, you know all about Battleships and are, understandably, a bit bored with it. Time to do something about that.

Start by keeping the same-sized grid. Now introduce a little bit of realism. You wouldn't really have the same fire power if half your fleet was sunk, would you? So allocate guns to ships – and specifically to squares within ships – and your salvo each turn equates to the number of guns you have remaining. Battleships is a game of honour: you must announce hits though of course if you want to cheat that's your affair.

Now let us see what else we can do. How about a depth charge? We can say that a depth

Figure 1

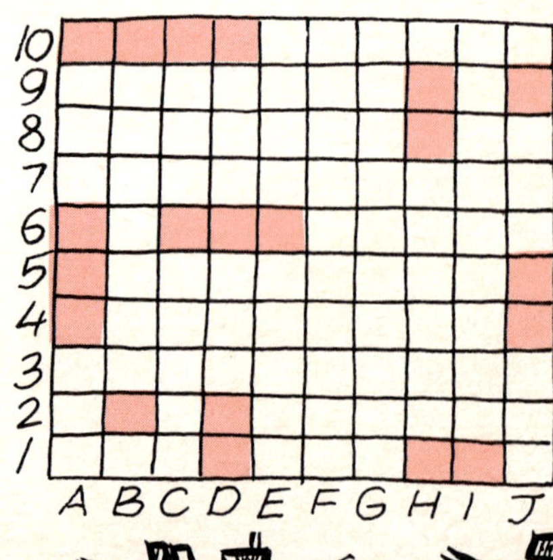

charge is effective on the nominated square and all the squares immediately round it (eight if away from the edge of the board). Allocate two depth charges per player to be used at any time in the game.

Another idea is to have a reconnaissance plane or searchlight which travels the full length of the area (10 squares horizontally or vertically). Two flights allowed in a game. Second player announces 'Destroyer and submarine spotted' but does not say on which squares.

These are quite simple things you can do to make Battleships more entertaining. As I said, there is no limit though if you get too sophisticated you will need a larger grid.

Hint

Don't bunch your shots, and eliminate all the squares surrounding the ships you locate since they must be unoccupied.

Figure 2

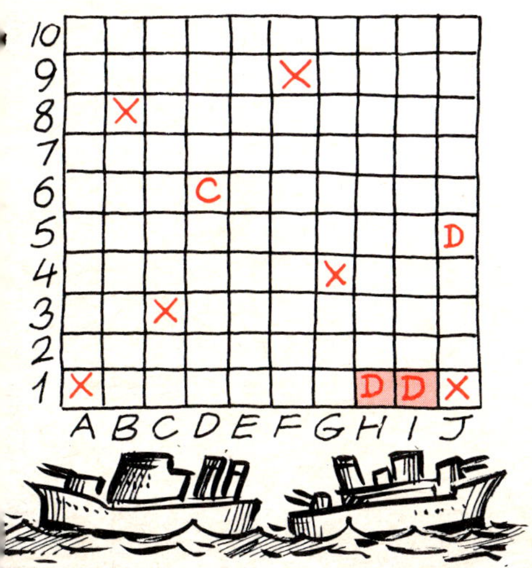

2 PEOPLE

SIM

This brief and essentially simple game is intriguing because no-one has discovered whether or not it is an advantage to start. That may sound incredible and perhaps it is. Anyway, what is certainly known is that a draw is impossible: one side must win.

Six dots are drawn on a piece of paper, each dot corresponding to the corner of a hexagon. If hexagons are all Greek to you, then draw a circle and mark in dots on the circumference that correspond to the even hours of a clock face (12 o'clock, 2 o'clock etc.).

Players in turn join any two dots with a straight line but no link may be repeated. That means that there are a maximum of 15 lines possible. Different coloured pens should be used so that the authorship of each line is immediately apparent. In a crisis – for example, where you only have one pen between you – one player should draw dotted lines.

The aim is to force your opponent to complete a triangle of his own colour in which the apexes are three of the six original dots. Triangles formed by crossing lines don't count. The first player to form a triangle in this way is the loser. In figure 1 you see a completed game won by Black.

Hint

Sorry, none available. There are conflicting views on how best to play the game. There are of course only three distinct opening moves.

Figure 1

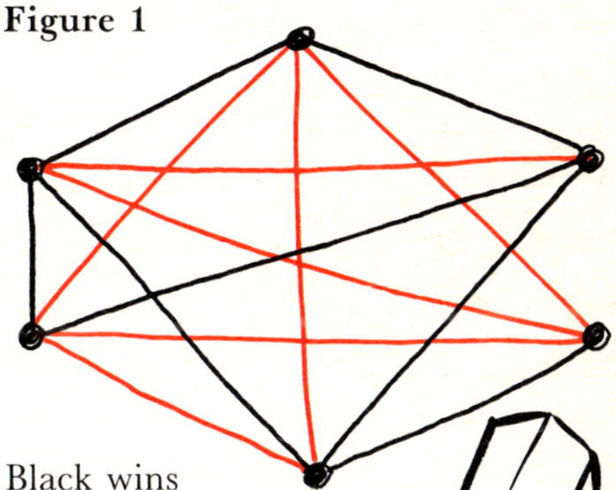

Black wins

PENCIL AND PAPER

2 PEOPLE

SPROUTS

Sprouts is described as a topological game. It is well described, for topology is that branch of geometry that concerns itself with the properties of a figure which remain unchanged when distorted; and that is exactly what happens in Sprouts. The contorted lines you draw do not affect the outcome of the game but they do give you scope for artistry so that apart from having a well-contested game you can also have one that is aesthetically pleasing – Sprouts has a visual bonus, so to speak.

You start with a sheet of paper – a large sheet if you want a long game or have ambitions to get hung in the Tate Gallery. On this you draw a few dots at random – we'll choose five. It is better if they are not too close together. As an estimate of how long a game will take, the number of turns cannot exceed three times less one the number of dots, so a five-point game cannot take more than 14 turns.

To begin, one player draws a continuous line starting and finishing at a dot. The line can be as straight or as devious as the player wishes and can start and finish at the same dot. The player then makes a new dot somewhere along this line and his turn ends.

There are only two prohibitions: a line may not cross itself or any other line and no dot (point) may have more than three lines extending from it. In drawing a line, you may not travel *through* a point since the first point you connect to your starting point terminates the line. Each turn reduces the number of possible connections by at least one, for the point added already has two connections (since it is on a line) so only one new connection is contributed, and that assuming that it can be used, whereas drawing the line removes two connections.

The first player who cannot draw a line when it is his turn, or declines to draw one, loses the game. Figure 1 shows a completed game which Black has won. Figure 2 illustrates some illegal plays.

Figure 1

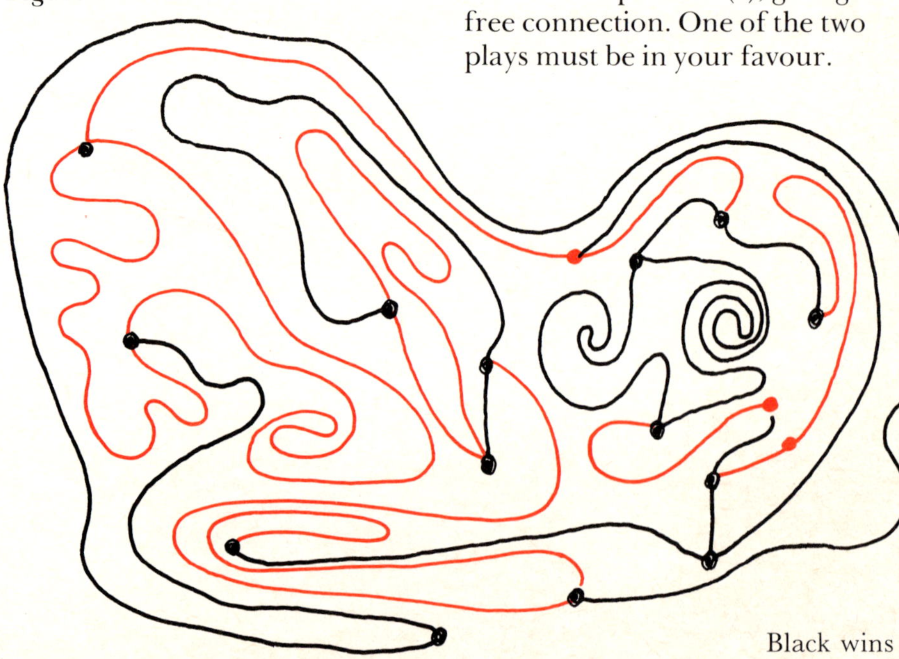

Black wins

Hint

If you are first player, you will want the game to finish with an odd number of lines; if you are the second player, then you will seek an even number of lines. Try to count ahead to see whether the number of connections remaining is going to work out in your favour. If not, then try to isolate a connection so that it cannot be used, so turning the game to your advantage. Consider figure 3. If it is your play in position (a), and you play as in position (b), then the point in the centre can never be used as there is no connection to which it can be linked and it cannot be joined to itself because it already has two connections. Alternatively, you could in position (a) have played as shown in position (c), giving a free connection. One of the two plays must be in your favour.

PSYCHOLOGICAL

2 PEOPLE

THINK OF A NUMBER

One player thinks of a whole number between 1 and 100 (or 1 and 200 if you want to complicate it) and the second player tries to deduce the number in as few questions as possible. Each question must have a Yes or No answer.

Thus, supposing the number chosen was 57:

Question
1. Is it divisible by 10?
   No
2. Is it more than 50?
   Yes
3. Is it divisible by 3?
   Yes
4. Is it divisible by 6?
   No
7. Is it over 75?
   No
8. Is it 63?
   No
9. Is it 51?
   No
10. Is it 57?
    Yes

Other typical questions are:

Is it an even number?

Is it a prime number?

Is the first digit higher than the second?

The game can be played by any number of players; one thinking of a number and the others playing as a team and asking questions in turn.

Figure 2

Illegal plays

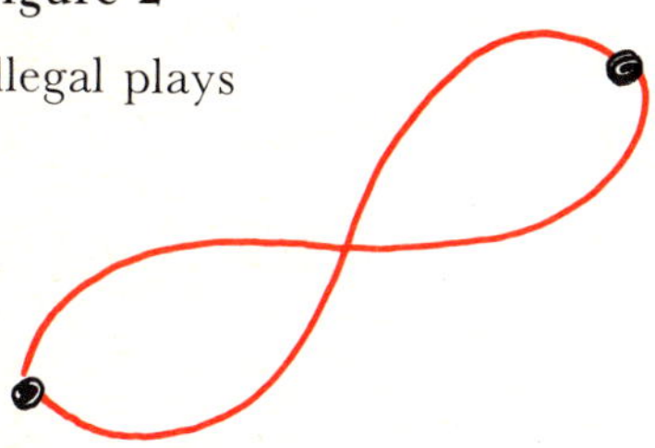

Line crosses itself

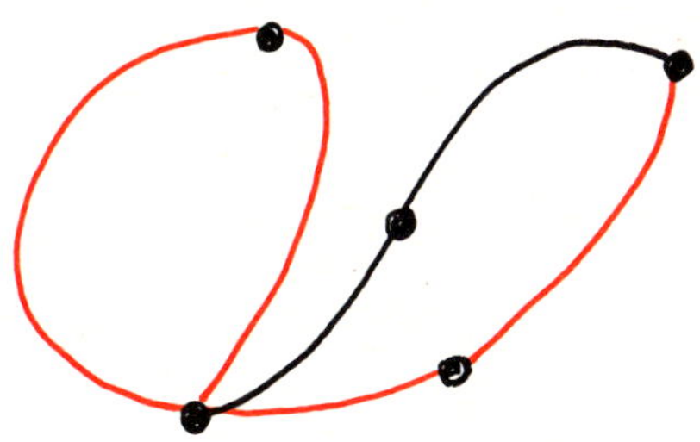

Four connections to one point

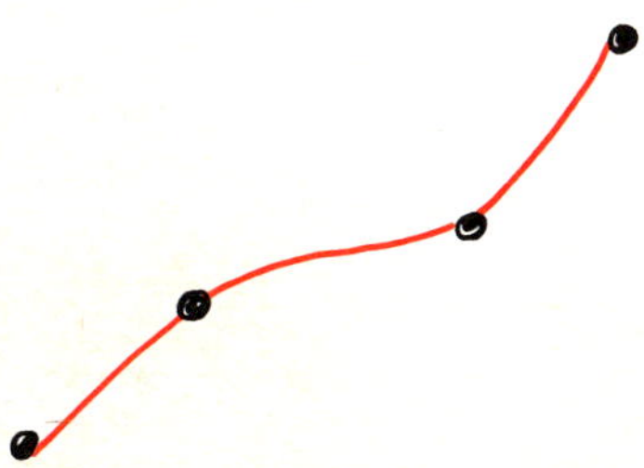

Line passes through intermediate point

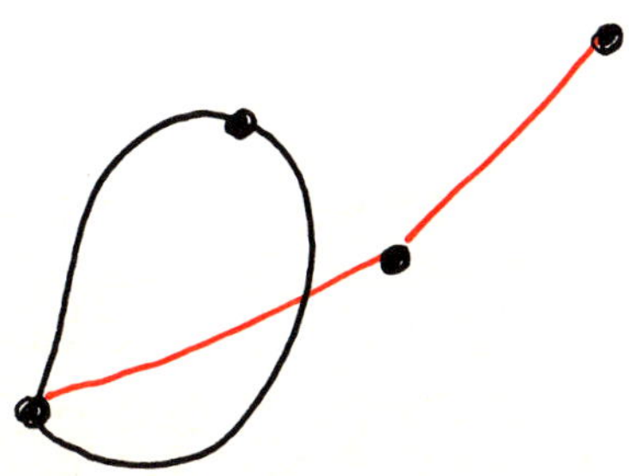

Line crosses another line

Figure 3

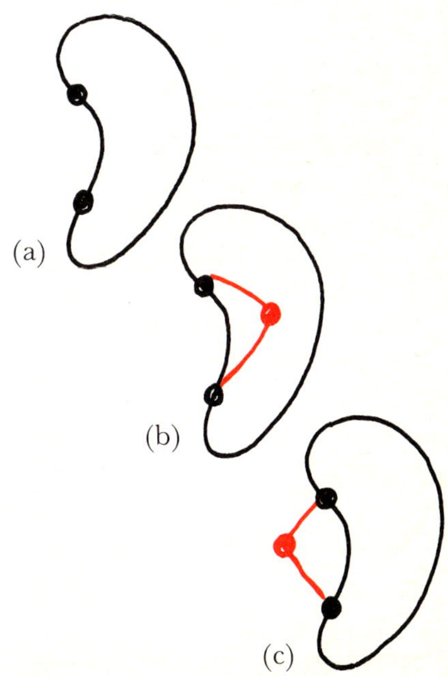

2 PEOPLE

FORTS

This variation of Battleships was invented by Harry Woolerton. Each player draws two 10 × 10 grids on a sheet of paper which he keeps concealed from his opponent. An agreed notation is marked on the grids for ease of reference. The grids represent desert areas. On one of his grids, a player marks three forts. A fort covers nine cells in the form of a square. Forts cannot overlap nor can they touch one another, even at the corners. A typical deployment is shown in figure 1.

When both players have positioned their forts they take it in turns to conduct 'bombing runs' over the other's territory. A run may be vertical, horizontal or diagonal. You execute a run simply by naming a perimeter square and a direction. For example, you might call 'A 10 south-east'. This means the bomber has flown down the long diagonal from A10 to J1. The defending player compares this with his deployment grid and announces how many hits, if any, have been registered on his forts. He does not say how many forts are involved nor in which cells the hits were recorded.

When a player is confident that he knows the locations of the three enemy forts he announces the cordinates of the centre cell of each fort; these are, in the imagery of the game, the headquarters buildings. If he is correct, he has won the game but if any cell he announces is not a headquarters building, then he has lost the game.

There is both luck and skill in the game – but mostly skill. The bombing runs must be picked with great care to yield the maximum information. Notice that whereas an orthogonal run always covers 10 squares, a diagonal run can be as short as two squares (e.g., 'B1 north-west').

As in Battleships, players use their second grids to record the results of their attacks. A good way to do this is to draw a line through each cell of a run and make a note of the number of hits beside the grid.
To give you some idea of the potential of the game, look at figure 2 which records the results of six bombing runs during the course of a game. The number of hits on forts are recorded by the figures in the circles.

It is possible from this intelligence to be precise about the locations of the forts and so win the game. Headquarters buildings must be in cells c9, d3 and h7.

Figure 1

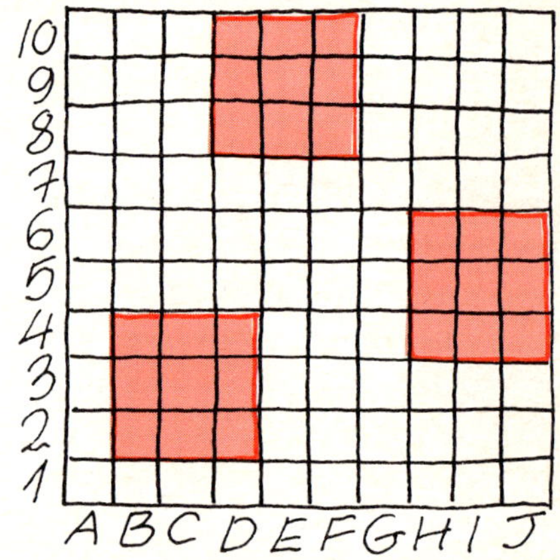

A typical deployment

Figure 2

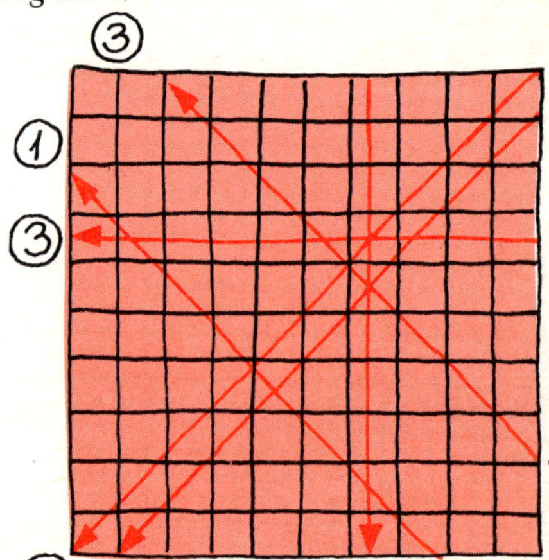

Bombing runs and scores

Hint

The maximum hits you can score on an orthogonal run is 6, the maximum on a long diagonal (8 squares) is 8. You can only ever score 3 hits on a fort with an orthogonal run so only two scores are possible: 3 or 6. With the diagonal run however you can score any number of hits between 1 and 8. About half a dozen runs are usually required to place the forts with certainty, but that assumes you are making use of the information the runs provide.

2 PEOPLE

FOUR IN A ROW

This is the Scotsman's version of a commercial game – so it is saving you £££.
You will need some squared paper to start with. Mark a base line seven squares long. Draw eight vertical lines from the baseline, each seven squares high and one square wide giving you 49 squares in seven columns of seven.

Pick your symbols, or better, colours, and take it in turns to mark a vacant square. It doesn't matter what marks you use so long as the two sides are distinguishable. The square marked must always be the lowest vacant square of its column – you can never leave gaps. Thus to begin you have the choice of any of the seven squares immediately above the baseline. Thereafter you must play at the bottom of an unoccupied column or in the square immediately above the last marked square of an occupied column. You will therefore continue to have a choice of seven moves each turn until the first column is full when your choice will be reduced to six, and so on. That is if the game isn't over by then. The aim is to get four of your marks in a row, vertically, horizontally or diagonally. Draws are possible but are unlikely. A finished game is shown in figure 1. Red has won.

Hint

It is an advantage to start. Straightforward moves are usually unavailing; try to set up positions in which threats can be mounted in several directions.

Figure 1

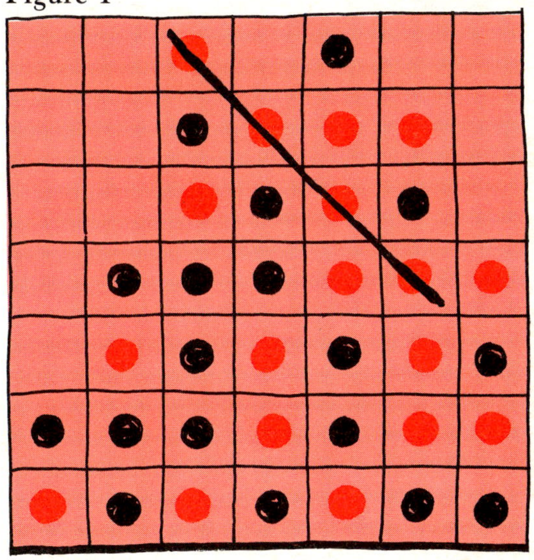

Red wins

2 PEOPLE

BOXES

Boxes is one of half-a-dozen games that everyone knows. You draw a grid of dots of any convenient size – say 10 × 10 – when players take it in turns to join any two adjacent dots either vertically or horizontally (but you can't join the same pair of dots twice). The aim is to enclose squares – make boxes if you like – and every time a player does so (by adding the fourth side to a box which already has three sides) he puts his initial inside and gets another turn. The player who owns most boxes when the grid is completed is the winner. You can never pass your turn! What usually happens is that nothing much happens for most of the game while players laboriously manufacture two-sided boxes. Eventually one player has to draw in a third side and the game finishes in two or three short bursts in which boxes multiply like price rises. A section of the grid in the course of a game is shown in figure 1 in case you are in any doubt about what the game looks like.

A child's game you say, but here's an interesting thought. While computers are perfectly able to master easy games like Chess and Bridge, or compute the population of China, none can yet play an intelligent game of Boxes. Of course, they can play the game but they are not much better at it than you or I. The reason is quite simple: since no-one has been able to plumb the game's strategy, no-one has been able to write a sensible computer program for it. Boxes is a game of pure skill so it must be an advantage or disadvantage to start, given the grid size, but nobody knows which. If you have a bit of time to spare you could set about the task of establishing a few precepts for good play, but for the rest of you I'll suggest one or two embellishments you can introduce to make the game more interesting.

One rule, not commonly played, is that it is *not* compulsory to win a box. This can have important implications in some situations.

Trevor Truran had the bright idea of introducing a new element to the game that strictly limits the choice of plays. One player agrees to take rows, the other columns. The first player puts a token beside any row; the second player then places a token at the foot of any column. The row and column intersect at a point, and the second player (who is the first player to make a line) now joins it to an adjacent point of his choice, just as in the ordinary game. The first player now moves his token to another row and similarly links the point of intersection with an adjacent point, and so on (figure 2). You must move your token before you play so two consecutive lines can never be drawn from the same point. Boxes are formed in the usual way and earn an extra turn – again, the player must move his token before drawing another line.

If a player is unable to play because all the points along his opponent's line are full, then he must move to allow his opponent to play on the next turn; so by a bit of clever planning you can

Figure 1

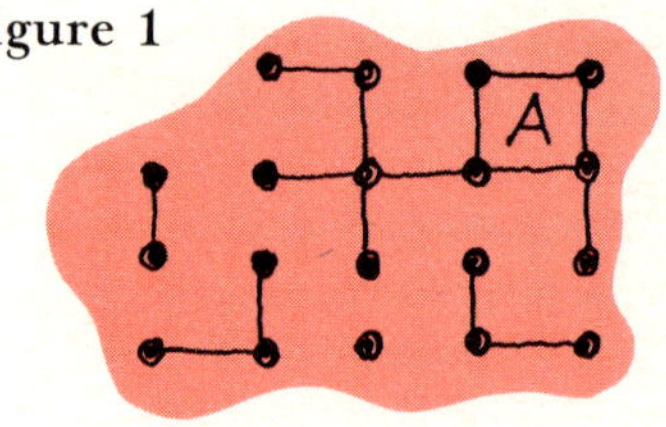

A game in progress (part of grid)

Figure 2

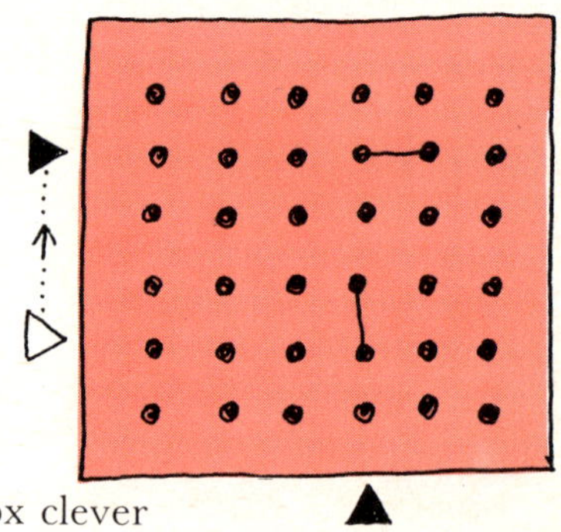

Box clever

Figure 3

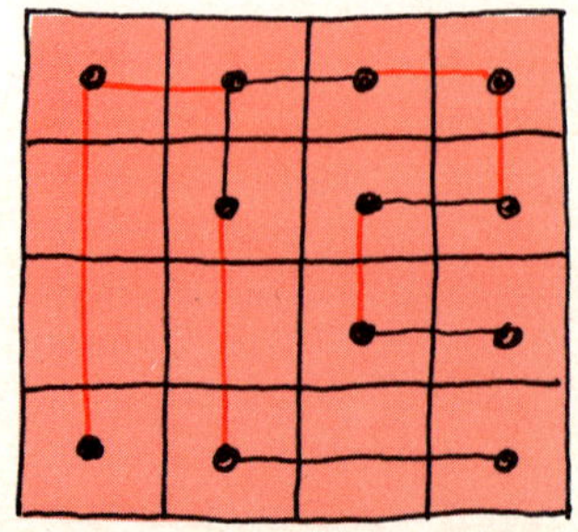

Whoever plays loses

earn yourself extra turns – if you want them, that is! Winner is determined as in the basic game. This variant, called Box Clever, has the merit of player interaction: you inevitably influence each other's moves.

Doug Engel invented an interesting little game that could be classified as a variant of boxes although it is a game in its own right. You start with a small grid, say 4×4, and you take it in turns to draw a line from the centre of one cell to the centre of another. The line may pass through empty cells but it must not repeat any part of a line already drawn and it must be parallel to the grid – no diagonal lines allowed.

The first player to create an enclosure loses. Figure 3 should explain this. Whoever is to play now loses since he must inevitably make an enclosure. Notice that an enclosure can be any shape – the definition of an enclosure is a succession of lines which can be travelled round continuously.

BOARD GAME

2 PEOPLE

ALQUERQUE

Most people have never heard of this ancient Moorish game. Yet they should have, for some eight centuries ago an unknown gamesplayer, resident probably in the South of France, borrowed the jumping move from Alquerque and invented Draughts. It is unlikely that you will be able to buy an Alquerque board but a sheet of card is easily marked up, and for men – why not draughtsmen?

The initial position is shown in figure 1. No one is quite certain how the game was played but that may be a bit academic since it probably depended where and when you were living: suffice it that the rules here work.

Players take turns, either side starting. A move consists of displacing a man to an empty adjacent point along a line of the board; thus in the starting position there is a choice of four possible moves. Alternatively, an opponent's adjacent man can be jumped if the point immediately beyond it in a straight line is vacant. Further jumps may be made in the same manner provided it is the same man that is moved each time. Direction may be changed between jumps but a capture must always be along a line of the board. Captured men are removed from the game and the winner is the player who takes all the opposing men.

Hint

Concentrate your men in the centre of the board but guard against multiple captures.

Figure 1

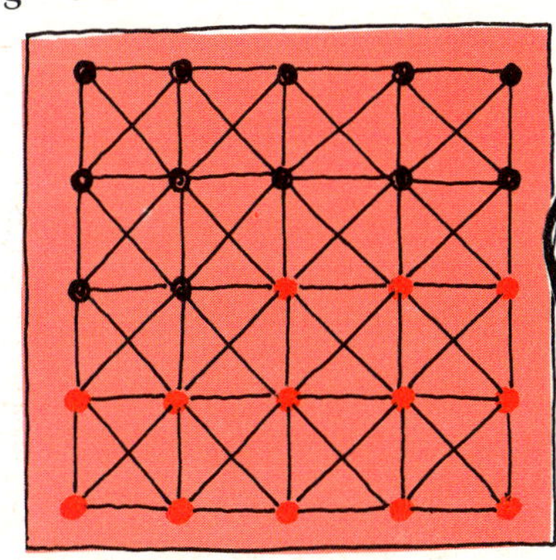

Starting position

2 PEOPLE

PASTA

You will need a Draughts set for this exciting little game. Starting position is as for Draughts (double corner on right) also the rules of play (and you know those, don't you?) except as modified below.

When you make a capture, instead of removing the captured man from the board you pick it up under yours. Subsequent captures are made in the same way, the column growing in size. However, when you jump a column of two or more men, either with a single man or a column of your own, you only take the top man with you. Of course, you can't jump your own men any more than you can in Draughts. As you can see, all the men stay on the board throughout the game.

Promotion is different also: when you have a column topped by two or more of your men, it may move and capture as a king – but watch out! your king may be demoted if your opponent leaps your column!

You win by moving a man or column to your opponent's first rank – the same move you would make to get a king in Draughts. Capturing is compulsory, so if your king reaches the back row with a capture and then has a further capture he must of course take it – and that doesn't win because your move didn't finish on the end rank. Pasta is full of surprises and it can take as little as a minute to play!

Figure 1

Starting position

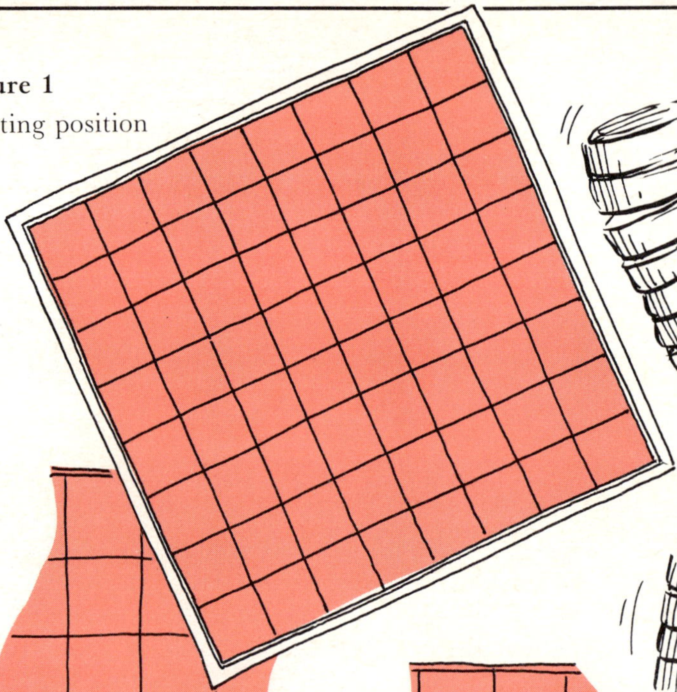

Figure 2

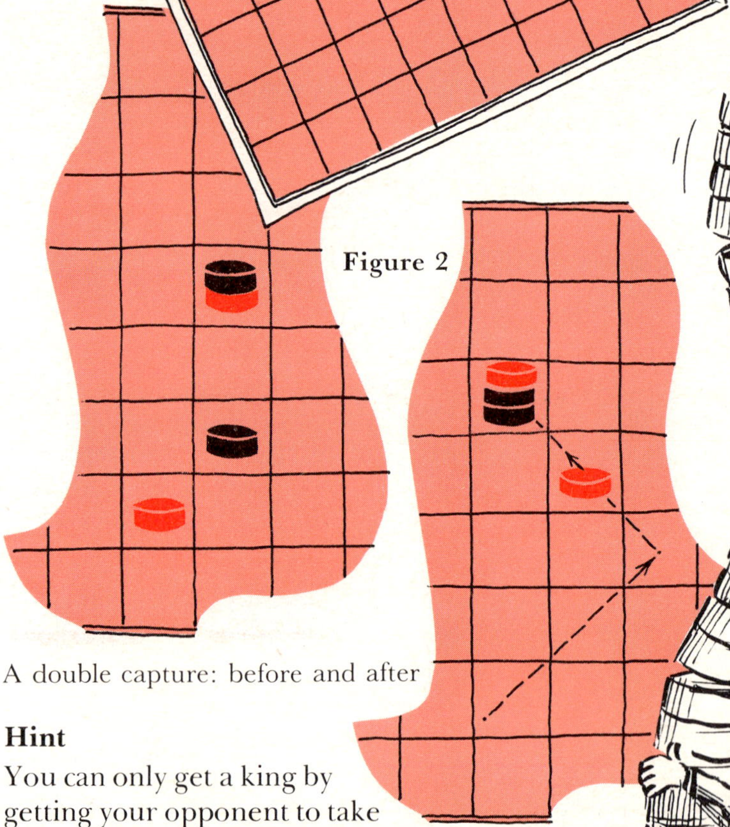

A double capture: before and after

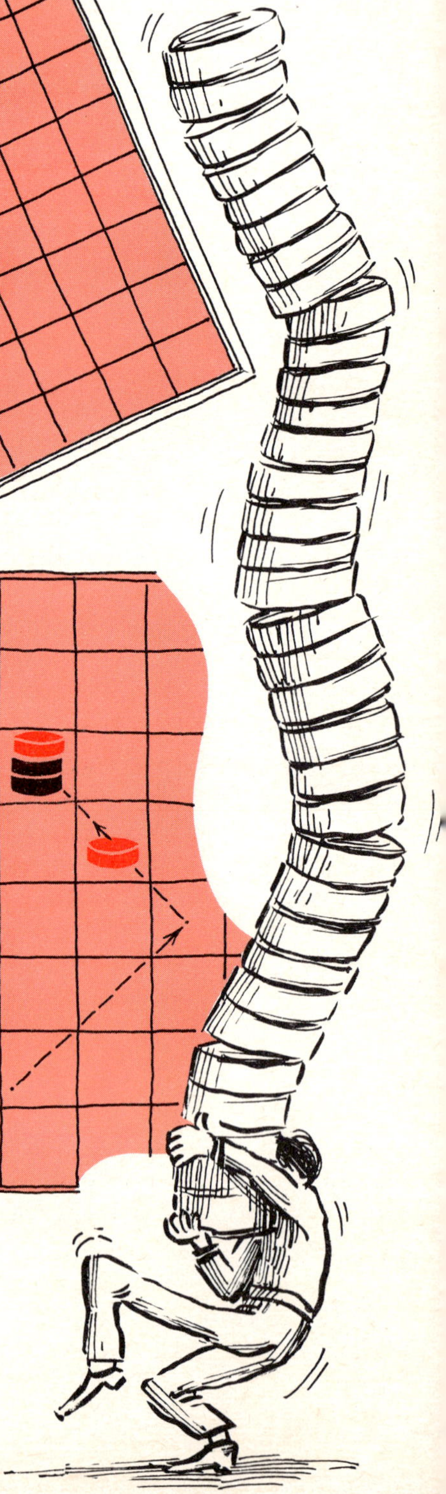

Hint

You can only get a king by getting your opponent to take your men and then capturing the top man off his column: a column always belongs to the side whose man is on top of it – columns can and do change sides often. So a crafty sacrifice or two can work wonders . . .

ANY NUMBER

PIG

This little game is ridiculously simple yet is still fun to play. All you need is a die (that's the singular of dice if by chance you didn't know).

A target total is agreed – say 100 or 250. Each player on his turn throws the die any number of times he likes. His score, which is accumulated, is the number of spots on the faces of the die – but if he throws a 1 his score for that turn is cancelled and the turn ends. Otherwise a player may end his turn when he pleases and pass the die to the next player. One round from a three-player game is shown in figure 1. A and C will add their totals to their previous scores.

The first player has the advantage in Pig so ideally everyone should have the same number of turns. But then the last player has the advantage because he will naturally play on to try and beat the leader. Best is to play the same number of games that there are players with each player starting a game in turn.

Figure 1

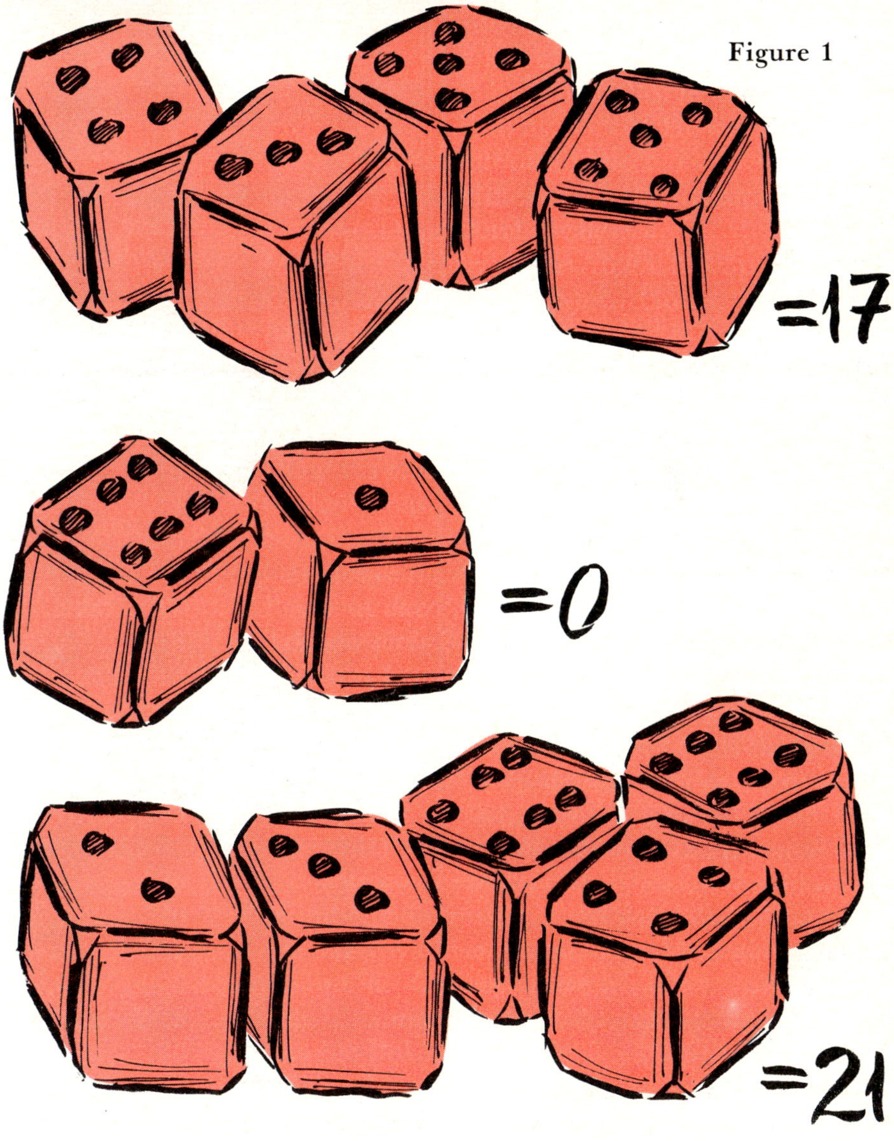

Hint

There is no skill in Pig but a little judgment is called for. Be content to keep your nose in front, particularly if you are last player – don't be greedy.

2 OR 3 PEOPLE

GOPS

This unusual little card game cannot be put into a convenient pigeon hole. It is part a gambling game (though there is absolutely no need to play for money), part an exercise in calculation and part a contest of bluff. You may tire of it after five minutes, but you will return to it again.

A standard pack is used. Divide into suits and if only two are playing, discard one suit. Shuffle any suit and place it face down in a pile in the centre of table. The players take a suit each (13 cards) and these are their playing hands, from which you will have gathered that there is no distinction between the different suits.

Cards are valued according to rank; Ace is one, Two is two, and so on up to Jack (11), Queen (12) and King (13).

The top card of the face-down suit is turned over and each player must bid for it. A player bids by selecting a card from his hand that corresponds in points to the bid he wishes to make. Bid cards are kept concealed until players are ready when they are turned over simultaneously. The highest-ranking card wins, and the player concerned takes the exposed card from the table suit and puts it to one side as his property. The bid cards are left face up in front of the players and are not used again. Now the second card is turned up and again the players bid, the highest bid winning the card. If two (or sometimes even three, if three are playing) bid cards are equal winners, then no-one gets the face-up card, which is taken out of play or put at the bottom of the pack. The cards of the table suit are valued in the same way as the players' cards, and the aim is to have won the most points (which is not necessarily the same as winning the most cards) after the 13 auctions have been completed. A game in progress is shown in figure 1.

The logical bid on each turn is that of the value of the card being auctioned (if a Five is turned over, for example, a bid

Figure 1

A three-player game in progress

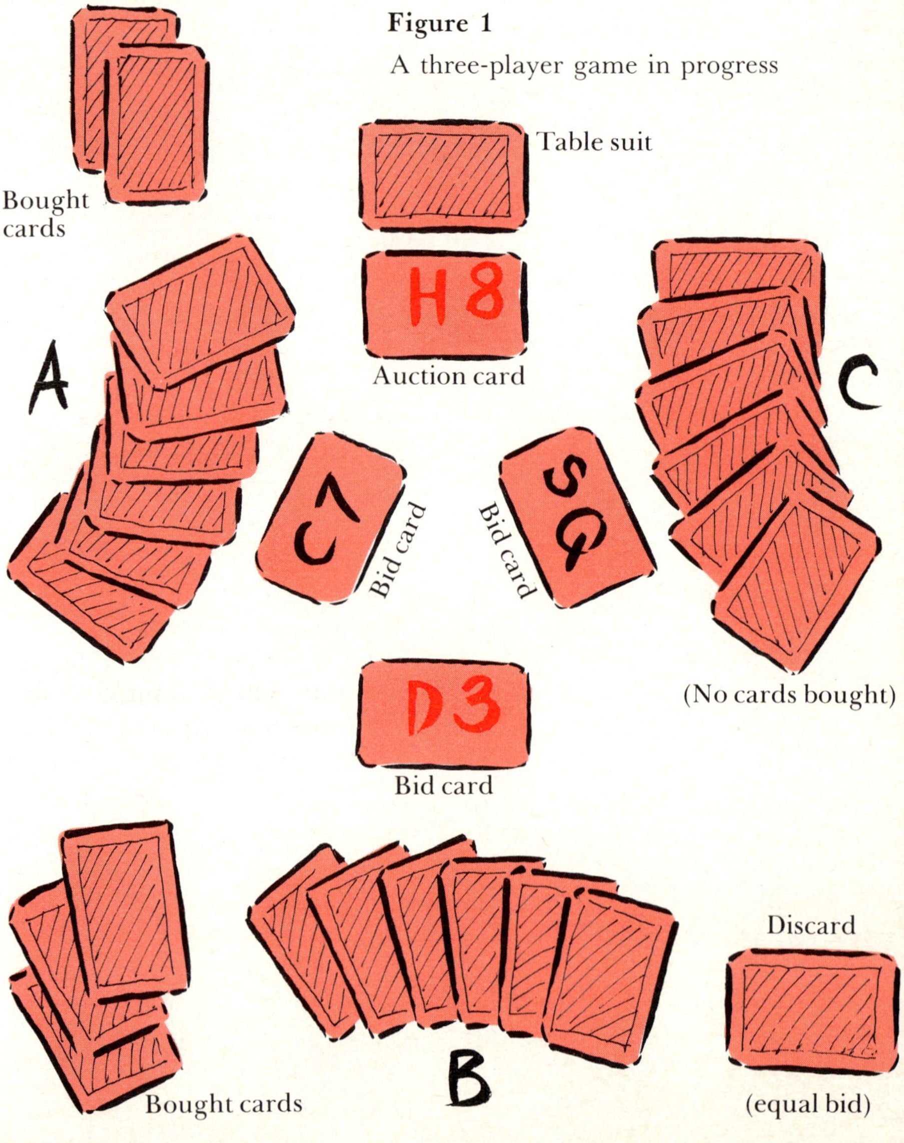

of Five) since a player's hand exactly parallels in value the table suit. However, for a number of reasons this is rarely the right bid.

Consider first the three-player game. This has an interesting element lacking in the two-player game which considerably influences the bidding. If you suspect that your rivals are bidding high (because there is a high-value card being auctioned) then by playing low you may be fortunate in that the other two have played identical cards, causing the auctioned to be cancelled. In this case you have put yourself in a strong position by conserving your points. To play Gops well, you must remember what the opposition has played so that you always know the composition of their hands and hence the possibilities open to them on a turn.

Gops is full of surprises and it is often not clear who has won until the last card has been played.

Hint

If you find it difficult to remember cards played, then try instead to keep in mind the cumulative totals (spent or remaining) of your opponents' hands which you can then compare with your cumulative total to determine your strategy at any given time. Every hand starts with 91 points.

BOARD GAME

2 PEOPLE

BAGH CHAL

This is a Nepalese game played in the valleys that cluster beneath Everest but is not played, as yet, in Evesham or Everton.

Draw a board like that in figure 1. In the four corners are placed four tigers. If you have difficulty finding that number or persuading them to take part, use coins or counters. The tigers belong to one player while the other player owns 20 goats, so you'll need 20 counters that can be distinguished from the tigers. You will now have recognized the game as a variation of Fox and Geese. Members of this family of hunt games are to be found all over the world in different guises.

After the tigers are in position, the player of the goats places one of his counters on any vacant intersection. Now the tiger player may move one of his big cats a single intersection; that is, along a line of the board to the next point. A tiger captures a goat by leaping over it, as in Draughts. The goat must be on an intersection adjacent to the tiger, and the point beyond must be vacant, such that the tiger, goat and vacant point occupy consecutive intersections on a straight line of the board. The player of the goats continues to add a goat at each turn but cannot move any. When all 20 goats have been placed (though their numbers may now be much diminished thanks to the appetites of the tigers) the goat player on his turn moves any one goat to any vacant intersection – in other words, a goat moves in the same way as a tiger. The tigers can continue to eat goats but the goats, logically enough, are forbidden to eat tigers. They can however smother them. If the goat player is able to hem in the tigers so that none of them can move, he wins. The tiger player wins by capturing all the goats.

Hint

It is impossible for the goat player to avoid losses in the early stages but he should try to keep the tigers out at the sides of the board where they are more easily contained. The tiger player by contrast should strive to occupy the points with most connections – notice that 5 have 8 connections and four have 5 connections. Here they will be hard to trap.

Figure 1

Starting position

4 PEOPLE

HIGHWAYMAN

Highwayman is a novel card game that you will look in vain for in card books.

A standard pack is used without jokers. Pip cards score their face value (Ace = 1 etc). Court cards do not score but have special roles:

Jacks are highwaymen
Queens are ladies
Kings are Bow Street Runners

The four players each pick or cut for suits – one suit for each player, who will be collecting the pip cards of it during the game.

Seven cards are dealt singly to each player, the remainder of the pack being placed face down in the centre of the table to form the stock. Players now examine their hands, when each player puts down in front of him, face to the table, all the pip cards he holds of the suit that he is collecting. This is the booty and earns points at the end of the game.

Elder hand (player to the left of dealer) starts. A player on his turn must do one of two things:

(1) Pick up a card from stock, adding it to his booty if it is a pip card of the chosen suit, otherwise adding it to hand; or

(2) Place a Jack face up in front of any player saying 'Stand and deliver clubs!' (or whatever suit it is the player is collecting).

A player who is 'held up' by a highwayman must take one of four possible courses of action:

(a) Hand over all the pip cards of the suit demanded, which the player of the highwayman adds to his booty, returning the Jack to his hand; or

(b) Play another Jack beside the first one saying 'I challenge you to a duel!' A 'fight' now takes place. Both cut the stock (or another pack if one is available); higher wins and the loser must pass over all the pip cards he holds in the suit the winner is collecting who then adds them to his booty. Both players retain their Jacks.
If the cut is equal, nothing happens and again both players retain their Jacks; or

(c) Play a Queen face up beside the Jack saying 'Spare a lady!' The highwayman, who is duly remorseful, is picked up and retained by the player of the Queen. The Queen remains on the table and is not used again; or

(d) Play a King face up on top of the Jack saying 'I arrest you in the name of the Law!' Both cards are then out of the game.

The game ends when one player has a full store of booty (Ace to 10 inclusive) or a player on his turn cannot play out a Jack when the stock is exhausted. Players now count up their booty. If a player has a full set, he scores 100 (pip-card count plus a 45 bonus). Play for a fixed time or to any agreed total.

Highwayman can be played with three. Include, but otherwise ignore, a fourth suit.

Hint

As only pip cards are added to the booty, players will tend to collect court cards in their hands as the game progresses, so if you pick up a Jack early in the game play it out before there are too many Kings and Queens around.

2 PEOPLE

CUTTING CORNERS

This superb little game is the creation of probably the best-known of all games inventors – Sid Sackson. You will need a large sheet of paper and two coloured pens, one for each player.

Start by drawing an ample square with two adjacent sides in one player's colour and the other two in the colour of the second player. One player starts by extending a perpendicular from one edge, making a right angle and dropping a perpendicular to an adjacent edge. We will call this line a bracket. The two edges must be of different colours. A position after the first player's turn in a game is shown in figure 1.

The second player now marks a similar bracket within the square but with one restriction: it must cross the first player's bracket once and once only. The restriction on joining two sides of the same colour, however, is lifted from here on.

The first player now draws another bracket. This bracket must make exactly two crossings, either of the same or different brackets. There is a new restriction: the bracket must *either* cross an opponent's bracket at least once *or* it must terminate on one of the opponent's edges. This is a minimum restriction: the first player for example could draw a bracket that crossed the second player's bracket and terminated on his edge.

The second player now makes a three-crossing bracket to the same rules, the first player a four-crossing bracket, and finally the second player makes a five-crossing bracket. A completed game is shown in figure 2.

The original square is now divided into a number of areas which may be squares, rectangles or many-sided figures. Each player now takes possession of all those areas that are made up of *more* sides of his own colour than than those of the opponent. He does this in the approved Boxes manner by putting a mark or his initial inside them. Areas that are shared – those that have an equal number of sides of each colour – are not counted. The winner is the player with the most areas.

The game illustrated in figure 2 is scored in figure 3. The second player has won by 7–5 with 10 areas neutral. (There will always be 22 areas in a game.)

Hint
Join different pairs of sides, not always the same pair as the first player did in the above game.

Figure 1

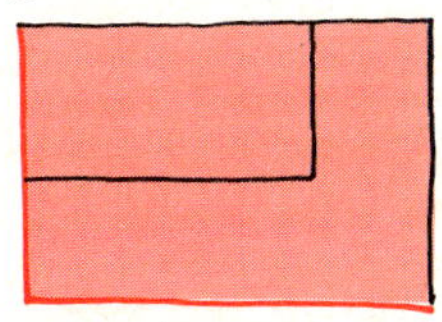

The first play

Figure 2

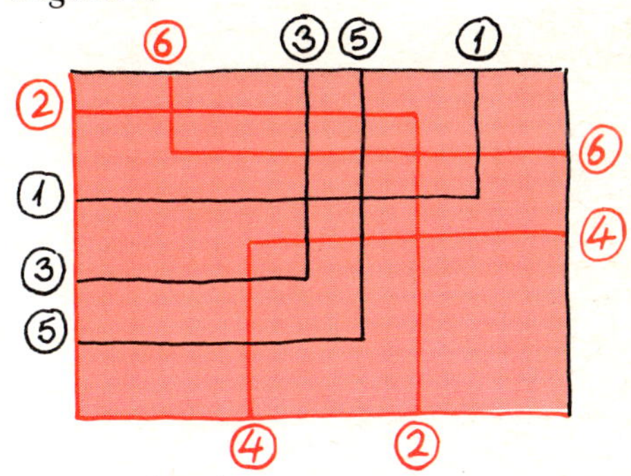

A completed game

Figure 3

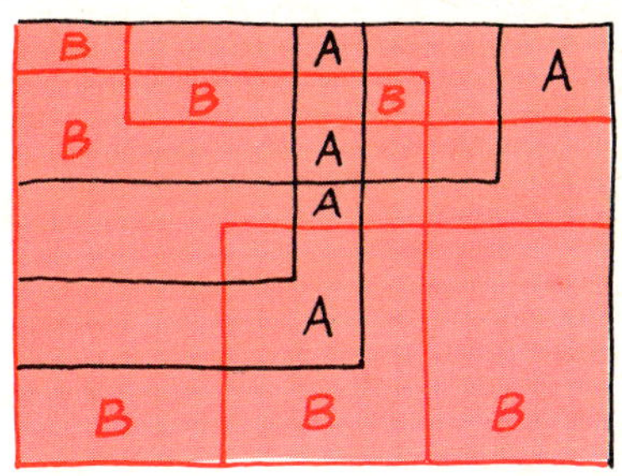

Scoring a game

2 PEOPLE

WHITE BOX

This splendid game was invented by Alan Parr and has proved popular in postal play. As its name suggests, it was inspired by Eric Solomon's commercial game, *Black Box*.

You have first to draw up a playing area in the form of a hexagon and then subdivide it into regular triangles, numbering these for reference (figure 1). This is probably the hardest, and certainly the most tedious, part of White Box. Since you will need two of these hexagons per game, it would be worth your while to draw several on a sheet which can then be photocopied.

Each player has his own hexagon which he keeps to himself. One player now shades in or otherwise marks a few triangles, which we will call mirrors, of his choice. The number must be agreed beforehand – try experimenting with 4, 5 or 6.

The task of the second player is to discover the exact whereabouts of these mirrors. He does this by injecting 'light rays' (a torch beam, if you like) into the hexagon. The first player consults his grid and informs the second player where the beams emerge. Where do they emerge? Well, if a beam does not strike a mirror it will simply come out the other side of the grid in a straight line. Beams are injected into the hexagon through the perimeter triangles and parallel to the lines of the grid; thus there are two possible directions for each triangle, and a glance at the diagram should clarify this. For ease of reference, these two directions are referred to as *a* and *b*; *a* always being the first direction, read clockwise.

In figure 2, the second player, who does not know the whereabouts of the four mirrors, might decide to inject a ray at 51a which he would do by simply giving the reference. In this example, the first player would reply '8b', meaning that the ray has emerged along the line 8b. The second player will mark his grid accordingly so that he can later make use of this intelligence.

What happens if a light ray strikes a mirror? 'The angle of incidence,' say the books on optics, 'is equal to the angle of refraction'. That means, in simple terms, that the ray is reflected at the same angle that it strikes the plane of the mirror, which is exactly how it behaves in White Box. Thus if a ray was injected at 49b it would be reflected by the mirror at 43 and emerge from the hexagon at 39b.

That is fairly straightforward. What happens then if the ray strikes a mirror, is reflected and then strikes a second mirror? And perhaps a third? Answer: the laws of optics are not changed; the ray continues to be reflected according to the same rule, and emerges from the hexagon somewhere. Thus if you injected a ray at 7a, it would strike the mirror at 43, be reflected up to the mirror at 20, across to the mirror at 22, down to the mirror at 48 and out at 17b. All you would be told is that the ray emerges at 17b.

Now to the scoring. You count 1 point for every ray you use. If you believe you know where the mirrors are, you announce the numbers of the triangles you think they occupy. If you are correct, then your score is the number of rays you used; if you are wrong, then you add 5 points to your score for every triangle that you misplaced. You now change roles for the second half of the match. The player with the fewer points is of course the winner.

Figure 1

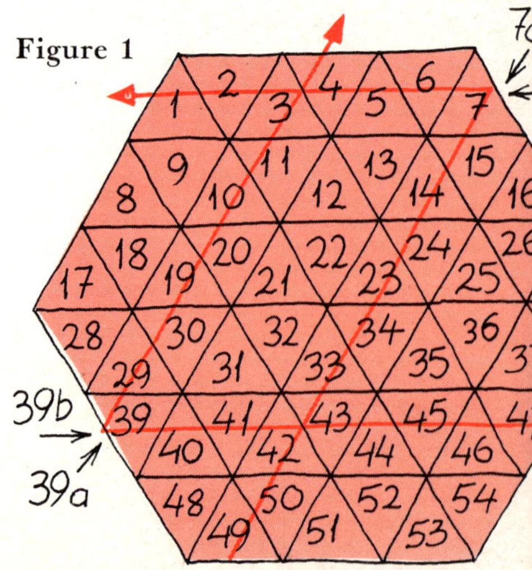

Playing area with notation marked

Hint

There is very little skill in positioning the mirrors. There is a great deal of skill in choosing where to inject rays; too much in fact to discuss here. It is worth noting that a ray which passes uninterrupted through the grid will emerge at a 'b' number if it was injected at an 'a' number and vice versa.

You can make the game a little harder by only announcing the number of the triangle where the beam comes out, omitting the direction.

Figure 2

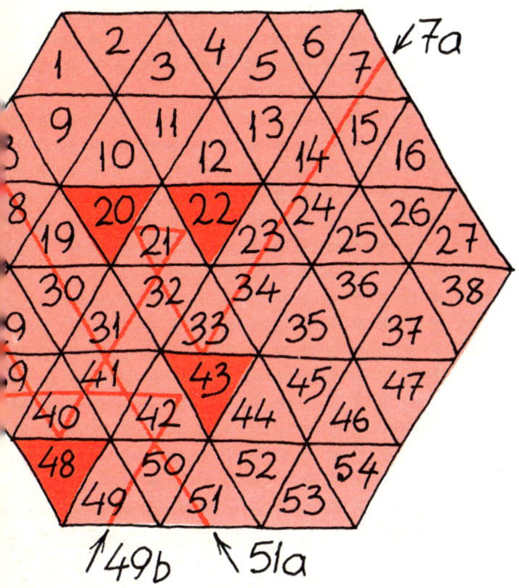

Game with four mirrors

2, 3 OR 4 PEOPLE

AUCTIONS

Auctions is fun as well as being quite skilful. It is best for four players. All you need is a standard pack of cards.

Start by dealing five cards singly to each player. The object is to get seven cards of the same suit (a flush) or a sequence (suits disregarded: ace high or low) in your own hand. You have only been dealt five? Never mind; you'll be getting more.

Elder or Eldest hand (that's the player on the left of the dealer – play is clockwise) takes one card off the top of the stockpile and adds it to his hand. The stockpile is the balance of the pack, face down in the centre of the table. Elder (or Eldest) now turns the next card over to form a discard pile. This card is auctioned with players bidding in turn. How do you pay? With cards from your hand (and of course of your choice). The possible bids are therefore 'No bid', 'One', 'Two' etc. If all no bid, the card is left and the next player draws. In the auction every player must either bid, and the bid must be higher than the previous bid, or pass ('No bid'). The auction can go round more than once; that is, a player who did not bid the first round can bid the second, or increase his bid. The auction is over when all have passed except the top bidder who then takes up the card and adds it to his hand at the same time discarding the number of cards he bid. These discards are put in the discard pile and may be examined at any time during the game by any player.

If no-one has got a flush or a sequence by the time the stockpile is exhausted, the discard pile is picked up, shuffled and placed face down to form the new stockpile, when play continues.

You can play an agreed number of rounds, the winner of each round earning one point. You don't score more if you get more than seven cards in a sequence but if the sequence is all of the same suit, award three points.

A refinement which adds to the skill of the game is to forbid payment by any card of the same suit or denomination as the auctioned card.

You can bid beyond your means if you like in order to force your opponents to bid higher, but if you are left with the bid then you are bankrupt and are out of the round.

Hint

The middle ranks are the most sought-after cards since they are required for any sequence. Don't overlook the tactic of bidding for a card you think the opponent wants, and later discarding it. The opposite ploy is to bluff bid to encourage someone to overbid you in the mistaken belief that you are about to go out.

WORD GAME

2 PEOPLE

ARROW WORDS

You need pencil and paper for this game. Players write down four letters in a line, two each alternately, so as to form a word which is then linked in letter sequence by arrows. Figure 1 should make this plain.

The object is to add a letter to the existing ones on your turn so as to form one or more new words, each word scoring the number of letters in it (five-letter word = 5 points). The player with the highest total score when no further letter can be added to form a new word is the winner (or the winner of that round if you are taken by the game and have more than five minutes to spare).

There are a number of restrictions:

(1) A letter may not be repeated;
(2) All letters must be linked to at least one other letter by an arrow but no letter may be linked to more than four other letters;
(3) A pair of letters linked by an arrow cannot subsequently be linked by an arrow in the opposite direction;
(4) No arrow may cross another.

That probably sounds a bit confusing and there is nothing better than an example to explain rules. Look now at figure 2. First player has put down a T and by inserting arrows he spells METAL (he cannot also score for MET) and MELT. By reversing the arrow between the E and L he could have spelt TALE instead of MELT. The play earns him nine points. He could have done better however by playing as in figure 3 where he scores for MALT, MATE, MEAT and TEAL (every word made must include the added letter, note) for 12 points.

Now it is the second player's turn and he adds an S (figure 4). He scores for MEALS, MELTS, METALS and SMELT – 21 points. Notice that he cannot score for SET or SEAL because the E already has four arrows attached to it. Can you find a better play?

Hint

Remember that you can place your additional letter anywhere on the paper. At times you will find that by choosing the location carefully you will be able to make a connection that would otherwise be closed to you because of the rule that forbids arrows to cross one another.

Figure 1

Figure 2

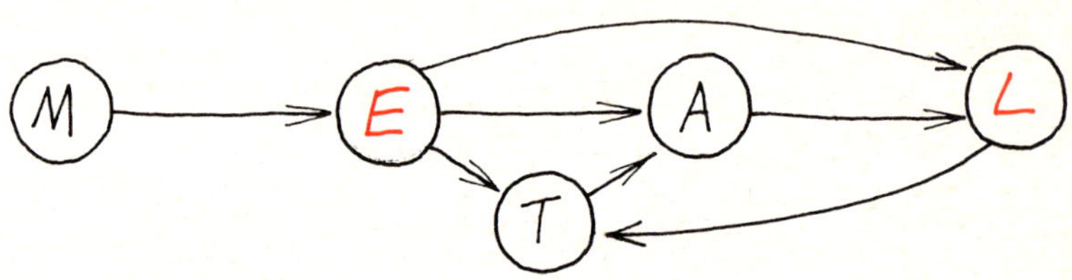

Figure 3

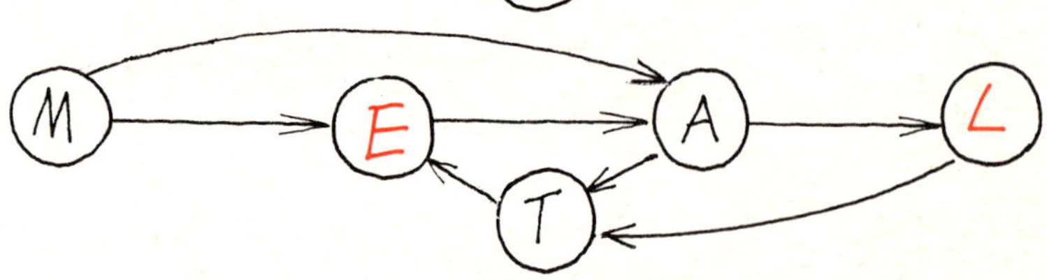

Figure 4

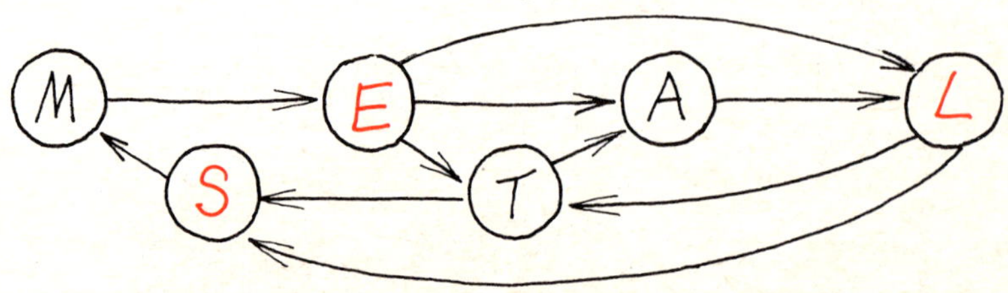

BOARD GAME

2 PEOPLE

BLITZ HALMA

Halma is a fine game if you happen to have a Halma set and an hour or two to spare. If all you have is a draughts set and five minutes to spare, try Blitz Halma, also known as Grasshopper.

Ten men a side are arranged as shown in figure 1. The board need not be chequered: if you don't have a draughts board, mark out a square on card.

Either side starts and the object is to be the first to occupy the opponent's base (starting position). Men move one square at a time in any direction including diagonally. A man may jump over an adjacent man *of either colour* to the square immediately beyond it in a straight line provided that the square is vacant and may continue to jump further men in the same manner all in the one turn, changing direction if necessary. Only one man is played on a turn and he may either move or jump, not both. All moves are optional which means for example that if a man can leap over six men in succession he can end his turn after leaping over, say, only three of them.

Having said that all moves are optional, there is in fact one exception: when one player has totally vacated his base, the other must, *on successive moves*, vacate his own base on penalty of losing the game. This rule is necessary to stop one player keeping a man at home and so preventing the other player winning.

Figure 1

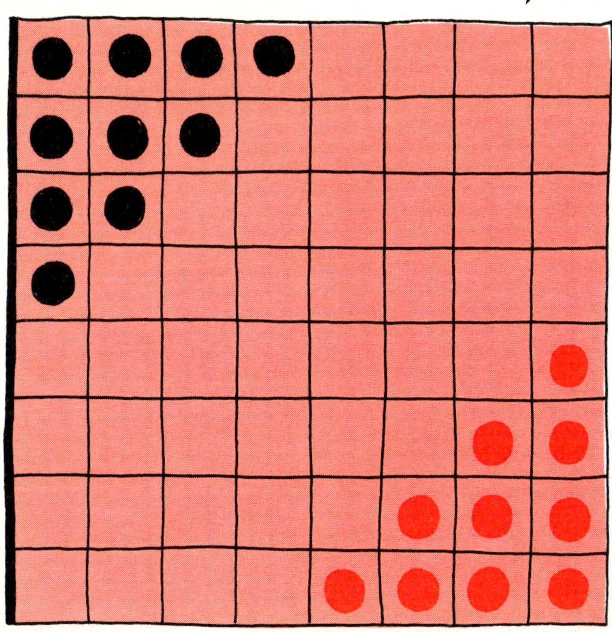

PENCIL AND PAPER

2 PEOPLE

AGGRESSION

There is nothing new about this game except that it may be new to you. If anyone had the time and interest they could probably write a book about its strategy so it's definitely not for simpletons.

Aggression, as its name implies, is a wargame. If you object in principle to wargames, you will probably be able to find another description for it – the mayhem, as will be seen, is very much in the abstract.

One player takes a large piece of paper and outlines an enclosed area. This represents a country and can be any shape – the odder the better. Ideally, it should not be too small as you'll have to write inside it; nor too large either because you'll need to get twenty of them on the sheet (this is a suggested number: try the game with less or more). The second player now outlines a second country which must border the first; the first player then draws a third country that must border either one or both of the other two. By the time 20 countries have been drawn you'll have a map looking something like that in figure 1. The countries have been lettered for convenience.

The next step is occupation. Each player has 100 armies to deploy. In this stage, players use pens of different colours or one player rings his entries. Taking turns, each player puts a number, representing armies, into any unoccupied country. This continues until both players have exhausted their entitlement or all countries are occupied. One player may elect to concentrate his forces in a few countries, quickly exhausting his 100 armies, while the other may elect to occupy a lot of countries each with a small garrison. It can happen that when deployment is complete there remain some unoccupied countries. A typical deployment is shown in figure 2.

The third phase is one of conflict. The first player (the same player plays first in each phase) neutralizes an opponent's country of his choice. A country is neutralized when the attacking side has a numerical superiority in a country or countries bordering it. A neutralized country is simply struck out while the attacker's forces are unaffected and may later take part in other attacks. The second player then neutralizes one of his opponent's countries on his turn and so on until all conflicts have been resolved (which may mean one player having several successive turns) when the winner is the player with most occupied countries regardless of the remaining strengths of the respective armies.

A local engagement is illustrated in figure 3. A first neutralizes B; then C, D and E combine to neutralize A (notice that C, D and E all border A so the play is legal). Now F & G combine to neutralize E leaving the position in figure 4. No further conflict is possible in this area as the antagonists have no common frontiers.

Figure 1

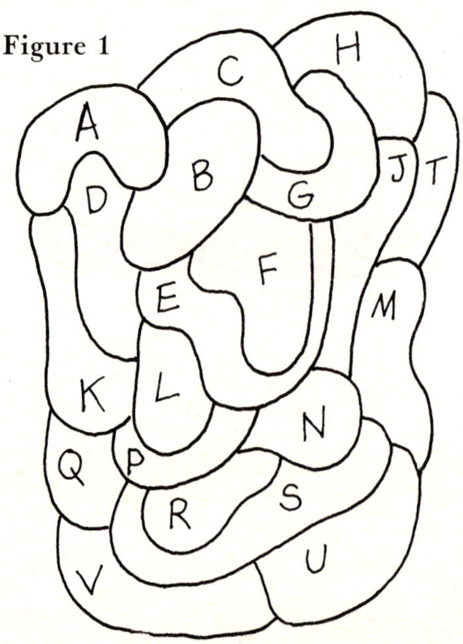

End of phase one (omitting I and O)

Figure 2

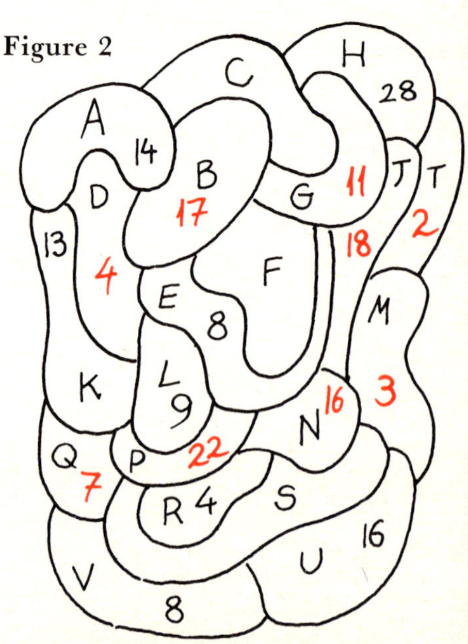

A typical deployment

Hint

Create buffer countries in phase 2 to shield countries with weak forces. During the conflict phase, first neutralize those countries that are able to combine to do you most harm. If you suspect that a certain country of yours is about to be eliminated, use it to neutralize an opponent's country while you can.

Figure 3

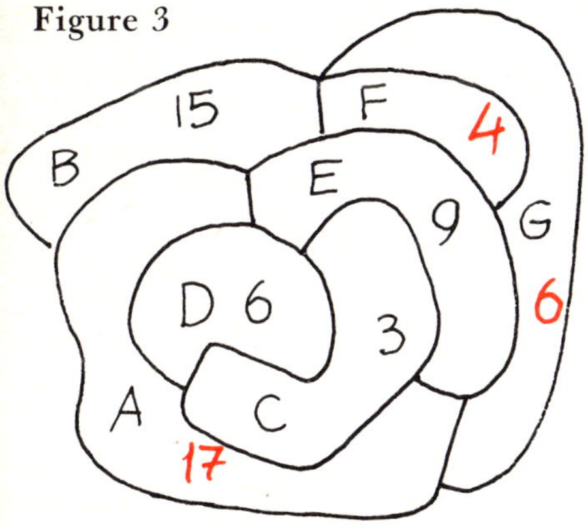

A local situation before phase three

Figure 4

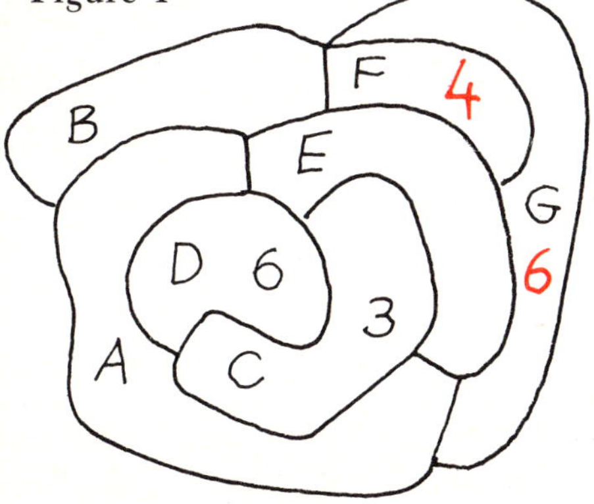

A local situation after phase three

BOARD GAME

2 PEOPLE

BULO

This game has been known for nearly fifty years – but only by the privileged few.

Draw a grid of 6× 6 squares or partly-screen a draughts-board. Place a counter in every square – 36 in all (figure 1).

Play alternates. At each turn, a player removes a counter or counters of his choice provided they are on the same line, either vertically or horizontally, and they stand adjacent one to the other – that is, there must be no gap in the line of counters removed. In the starting position, any number up to six counters may be removed from any row or column. Each player must pick up at least one counter on his turn, and counters picked up are out of the game. The player who picks up the last counter is the loser.

A simple example is shown in figure 2. First player wins by taking the two marked counters; any other choice loses.

Hint

You need to leave an odd number of isolated counters after your play in order to be sure of winning. But each line of two or more counters upsets this calculation since they can be converted into odd or even by taking selected counters, as in the example give.

You may recognize Bulo as a sophisticated version of Nim. If you can discover a winning strategy (and there must be one) the world would like to hear about it. No computer print-outs, please.

Figure 1

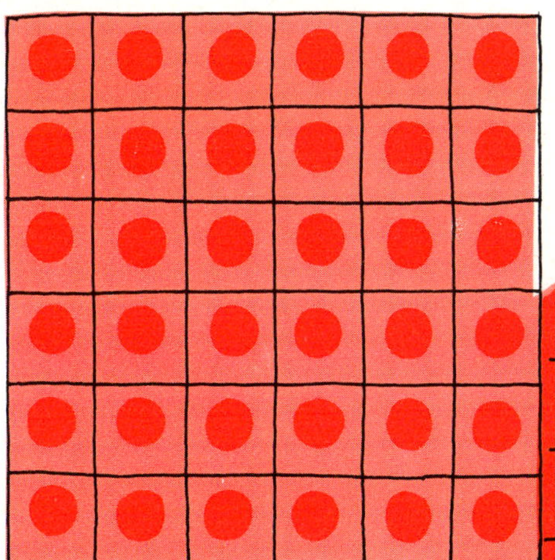

Starting position

Figure 2

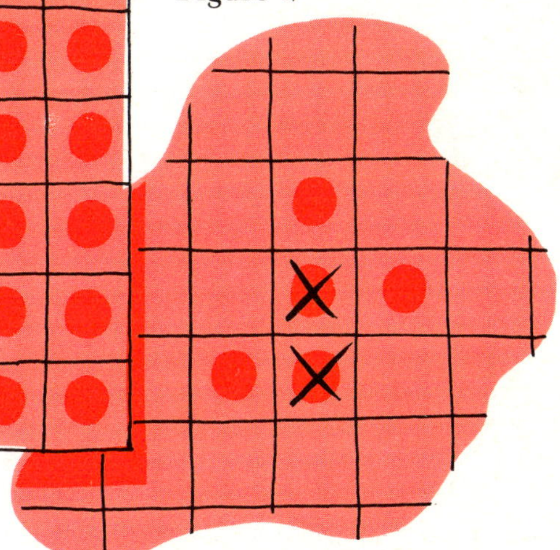

A game position

3 OR 4 PEOPLE

COLONIES

This game is not unlike Aggression but needs more players – three or four are best.

On a large sheet of paper each player in turn draws a small area to represent a country. An area can be any shape but each area after the first must border an existing one. There is one significant difference from Aggression: instead of creating a compact mass, a better game is had if a more diffused map is drawn.

When everyone has contributed eight or ten countries (prearrange the number to suit the company), the second phase begins. In this, each player in turn claims a country by putting his initial in it with the rule that countries with a common boundary may not be occupied by the same player.

When all possible countries have been claimed (players miss a turn if they have no legal move), a few unoccupied countries may remain – these will be the ones whose borders are shared by all the players so that no player can legally occupy them. A typical three-player game to this point is demonstrated in figure 1.

Now there is a new stage. Each player in turn tries to build a bridge between any two of his existing countries. This bridge is simply drawn as a line linking the two. No bridge however may cross another bridge nor may it cross any occupied country, though unoccupied countries may be crossed. Only one bridge may be built between each pair of countries. Subject to these restrictions, a country can have any number of bridges linking it to other countries and an unoccupied country can be crossed by any number of bridges, though obviously there are limits. Bridge building in a small sector is demonstrated in figure 2. Players miss their turn if they cannot make a bridge, and when all are finished the game is scored as 2 points per country plus 1 point for every bridge. The winner of course is the player with the highest score.

Hint

Offer to play first – it is a big advantage. A bit more balance can be achieved by reversing the order of play after phase 2, the player who started first in this phase being the last to play in phase 3.

Figure 1

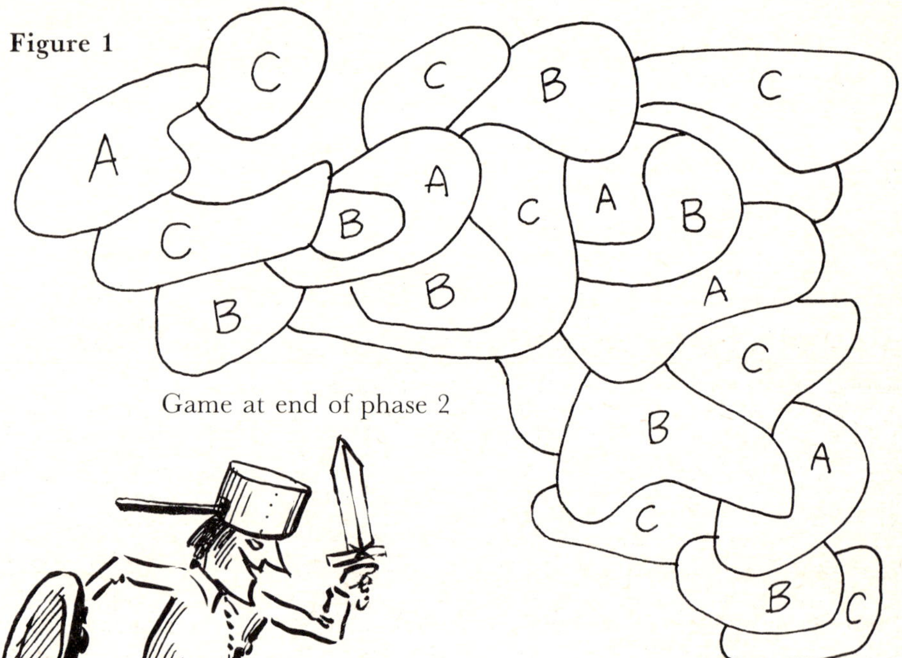

Game at end of phase 2

Figure 2

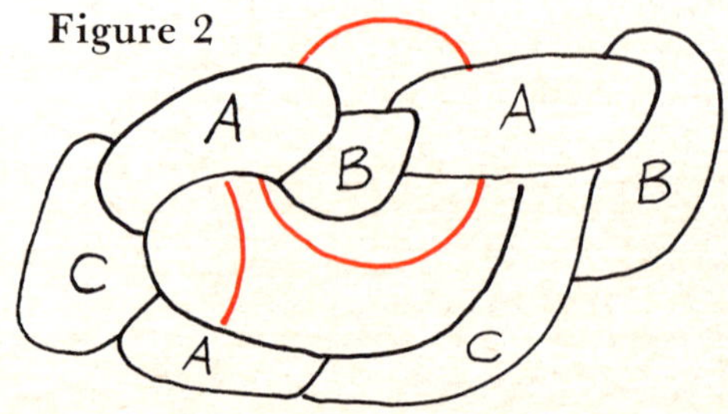

Building bridges

GALE

This game, which Martin Gardner calls Bridg-it is related to Hex but has one important distinction: each player uses a different grid.

Sixty dots are drawn in two staggered, but regular 6 × 5 arrays on a piece of paper. It is advisable that each grid is drawn in a different colour to avoid confusion, although this is not essential (see figure 1).

Each player on his turn unites two adjacent dots of his own colour with a straight line. The line must be vertical or horizontal, never diagonal, and it must not cross another line.

The aim of each player is to link any dot in the row of five at one end of his array to any one of the five dots in the row on the other side. Because of the way in which the arrays are constructed, this means that one player will be trying to unite top and bottom and the other left and right. The first player to achieve his aim wins the game, though it should be noticed that if one player achieves the union the second player will be unable to do so anyway.

The advantage to the first player, as in most games of this type, is considerable. Equality can be achieved by playing an even number of games, alternating the first move. Alternatively or additionally the first player can be banned from joining his two central dots on his first play. A game in progress is shown in figure 2.

Hint

Don't attempt to make a continuous line from the start: it is better to join strategic points across the grid and unite them only when your opponent is threatening to sever the connection.

Figure 1

Initial arrays

Figure 2

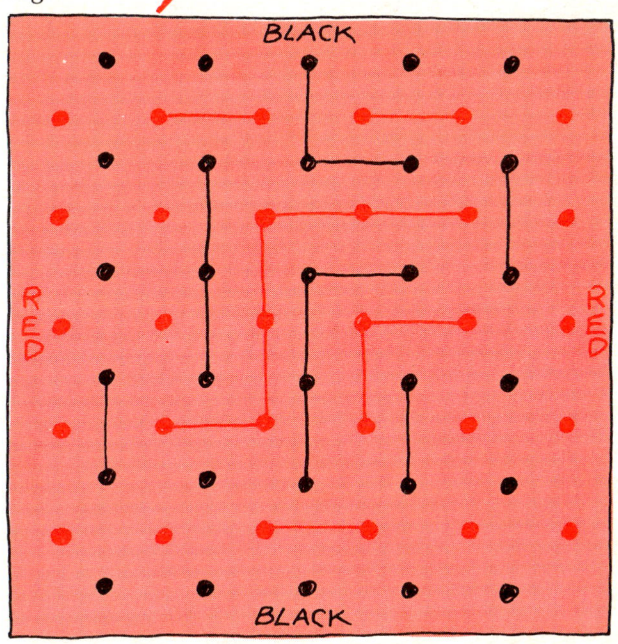

A game in progress

FENCES

This is not the easiest of games to understand but it is quick to play, skilful, and you won't find it in other books of games.

Start by drawing a grid of dots as for Boxes, but not so many. Give 6 × 6 a trial and see how it works out. A *square* in this game is the area bound by four adjacent dots – the same as a box in Boxes.

Players take contrasting symbols or colours. First player marks an EDGE square; second player now marks any vacant square, when the first player marks a second vacant square anywhere within the playing area provided it is in a straight line, either orthogonally or diagonally, with his first mark. The line must not pass through the second player's symbol. Having done that, he now draws one fence in the square of his first symbol, one in the square of his second symbol, and ONE IN EVERY SQUARE, IF ANY, BETWEEN THE TWO SYMBOLS. A fence is defined as a side of a square, a concept you are familiar with from Boxes. Notice that where the symbols are connected orthogonally, a fence may be common to two squares but this does not reduce the entitlement of one fence per square. Figure 1 may help you to understand this. A fence (side) has been drawn in each square (box) in which Red has a mark plus all the squares between them, a total of five in all.

Now the second player links his first symbol to a new one drawn in any vacant square in a straight line. However, it must not pass through any symbol nor may it pass through a fence at right angles or through a corner formed by two fences. It CAN pass through a fence diagonally.

Two more rules are necessary. You may not place a symbol in a vacant square unless it is possible to mark in a fence IN EVERY SQUARE along the straight line so formed. Finally, no fence may be erected by either side between two squares that are occupied by rival symbols. Figure 2 shows these various legal and illegal plays.

Figure 1

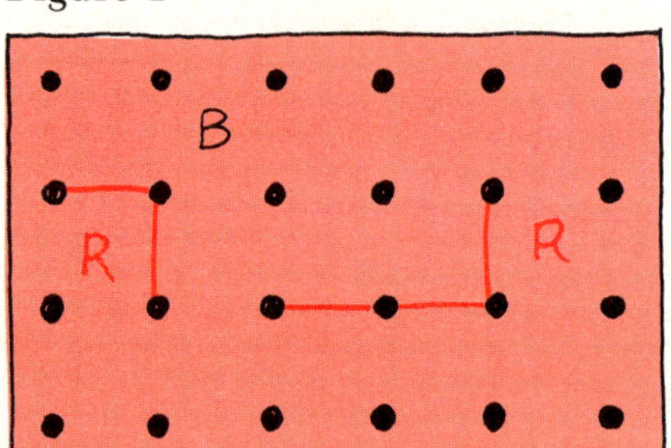

Two Red symbols in line with fence
entitlement added

Figure 2

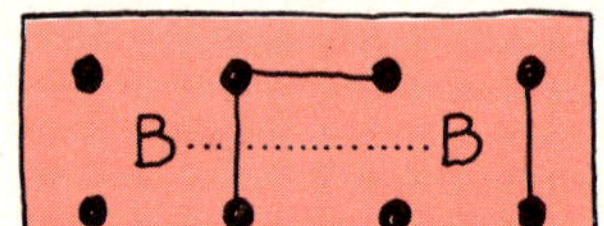

Illegal: line crosses fence at right angles

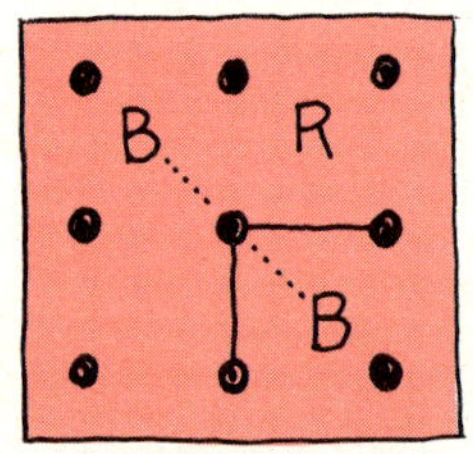

Illegal: line crosses enclosed corner

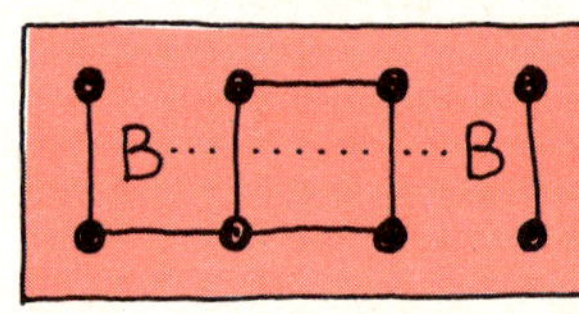

Illegal: fence cannot be marked in central square

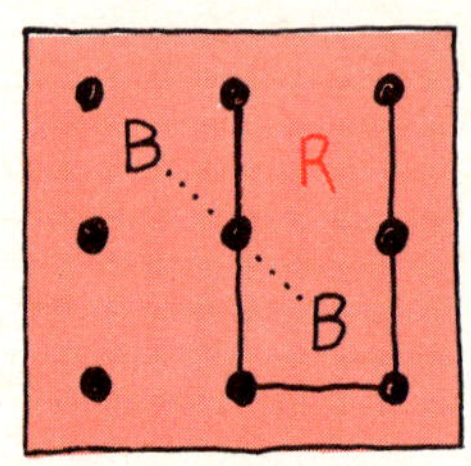

Illegal: only available fence in bottom square would divide rival symbols

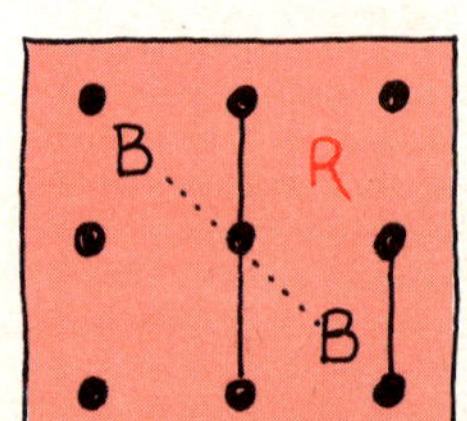

Legal: diagonal crossing of fence

Only now do we come to the object of the game which is to enclose areas with your own marker(s) inside plus empty squares. An area is two or more squares completely surrounded by fences.

The game ends when neither player can play or wishes to play (you can always forfeit your turn – and sometimes you may have to!). The winner is the player with most EMPTY squares in areas which he owns. He does not score for squares which have his symbol in them. Figure 3 shows a completed game. Black has won but typically the scores are low. Fences was conceived by Steve Peters and A. Sturmanis.

Figure 3

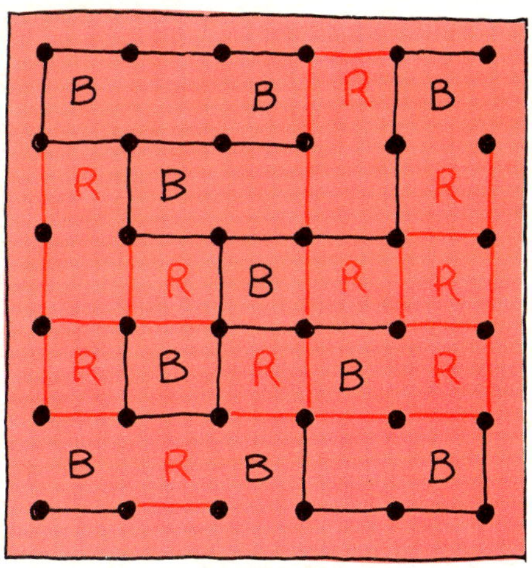

A completed game

PENCIL AND PAPER

2 PEOPLE

AMBUSH

This not-too-serious game is about cowboys and indians or, to be precise, about one cowboy (here in the role of a scout) and one indian.
The board is shown in figure 1 but you will need two boards, one for the scout and one for the indian. The scout's board is in full view of both players but the indian's board is screened and can be seen only by the player of the indian. The arrangement is shown in figure 2.

The scout starts at one end of the playing area and the indian at the other. Both move in the same way: from one intersection to the next along any line in any direction. The object of the scout is to reach alive any one of the three end vertices on the right; that is, the one the indian starts the game on and those on either side. The aim of the indian is to ambush the scout. You must move on your turn.

The indian moves first. The player of the indian makes a move on his screened board. For his first play, he has only a choice of two, but on his second play he will have six alternatives. The scout then moves openly on his board. Thus the indian always knows where the scout is, but the scout does not know where the indian is. If the scout moves to the point occupied by the indian he is said to be ambushed and the game is over. The indian may not attack the scout; that is, he may not move onto the point occupied by the scout; he must entice the scout into an ambush. As explained earlier, the scout has only to reach one of the end points to win but his survival chances are not particularly good.

Players should change sides after each game, a match consisting of any even number of games.

Hint

As the indian player, don't get too close to the scout to begin with: if the scout passes you you cannot stop him sprinting home. As the scout player, keep to the middle of the playing area where you have more options. If you believe you are level with the indian you cannot be intercepted provided you keep moving straight ahead.

Figure 1

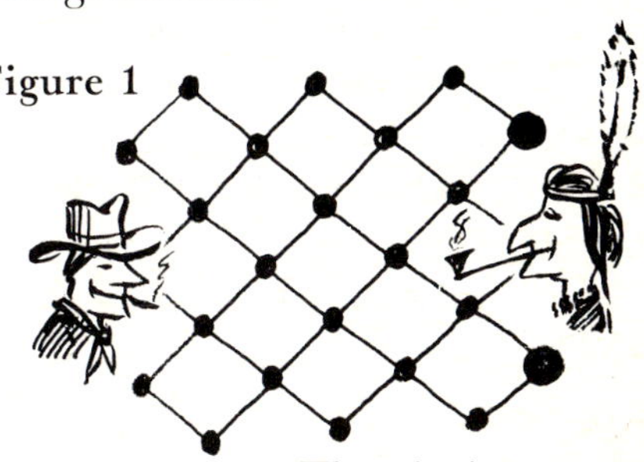

The playing area

Figure 2

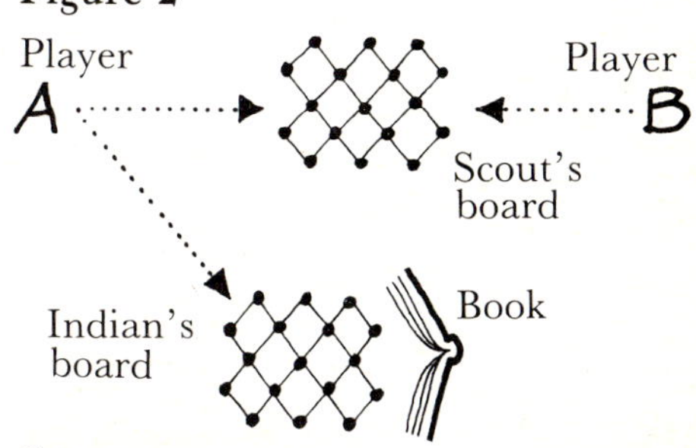

Suggested arrangement of boards

ANY NUMBER

GHOSTS

This game has been around for some time but keeps its popularity. If you are a crossword addict or have a good vocabulary, then Ghosts or one of its versions will probably appeal to you. On the other hand, if your mastery of the language is largely confined to one-syllable words you should move on to the next game.

Players take it in turns to announce a letter of the alphabet. The letters, taken in the sequence announced, should be capable of extension, by adding a further letter or letters, into a legitimate word. What is legitimate you must decide beforehand, but all words should be of at least three letters.

The object of the game is not to complete a word on your turn. For example, after the letters B, A, it is your turn. You announce 'G', with bagatelle, or perhaps baguette, or both, in mind. Unfortunately, you have completed a word – BAG – and so have lost a life. When you lose three lives you become a ghost and drop out of the game (or if you like, look on the words you think up as ghosts though they are a bit more like skeletons).

You may challenge or be challenged by anyone, and if a word consistent with the given letters cannot be named, then the player concerned loses a life, otherwise it is the challenger who does so.

Here is a sample game:

Player A: 'B'
(there are hundreds of words beginning with B: you don't need to bother to think of a word at this stage)
Player B: 'R'
(again, plenty of possible words)
Player C: 'O'
(now things are getting warmer: player C had BROTH and BROOM in mind, both of which would finish with player B, but overlooking BROOCH which would end with him)
Player A: 'N'
(with BRONCHITIS in mind, omitting to notice that the word would end with him)
Player B: 'Z'
(with BRONZE in mind: player B is fairly confident that this will make A lost a life)
Player C: 'I'
(player C can think of nothing and so decides to bluff: he cannot of course pass)
Player A: Challenge
(player A can think of nothing either but suspects he will be challenged by B)
– and player C loses a life, and starts the next word.

Hint
When your turn comes round try to think of a word, like BRONZE above, which will be predetermined by the next letter – the one you are about to announce.

Ghosts can be a bit limited. You can make the game more interesting by permitting letters to be added in front of the sequence but otherwise keeping the same rules.

Even better is Anaghost in which the letters can be jumbled – in other words, they can be in anagram form. Someone may have to write them down in this version since a number of random letters are not easy to retain in mind.

PENCIL AND PAPER

ANY NUMBER

SPOOF WORDS

If you don't know this game you may recognize it from a popular T.V. show for which it was modified.

You need a fairly large dictionary, a number of players armed with pencil and paper, and a devious turn of mind. Someone, who we'll call the selector, looks up an obscure word in the dictionary, which he thinks will be unfamiliar to the other players, and announces it. He then copies out the dictionary definition of the word or, if all agree, he can make a close paraphrase of it. Everyone else now writes down a plausible (though almost certainly erroneous) definition of the word. Definitions should be as credible as possible since that's the way you win.

All the definitions are passed to the selector who shuffles them in with the correct definition and then reads them out one by one giving each a number or letter for identification. The selector must be careful to keep the papers concealed and to read them all in the same tone so that he does not give himself or anyone else away.

The selector now asks each player in turn to cast a vote for the true definition. He then announces which definition was correct and awards 2 points to everyone who got it right. He also awards a point for every vote cast for a wrong definition to the player who devised it. The selector takes no part in the scoring though you can play the version where, if no-one gets the right answer, then the selector scores one point for every player taking part.

Hint

Try to construct your definitions in the style of the dictionary that is being used (a quick look through it beforehand should get you on the right lines).

If you haven't any idea which definition is correct you can always collect a point by voting for your own.

2 PEOPLE

GOLOMB'S GAME

Pentominoes are well known to those folk who dabble in recreational mathematics, elevated to a highly-respected science by Martin Gardner's column in the *Scientific American*.

You can buy sets of pentominoes quite cheaply but unfortunately some manufacturers give them other names so you may have trouble finding them. It is not necessary anyway: you can make you own out of cardboard or, if you are a handyman, out of some durable material. At a pinch, you can even use paper.

What *are* pentominoes you may now be asking? Simply, they are two-dimensional shapes that represent all the different ways that five identical squares can be assembled neatly (without bits sticking out). The easiest way to describe them is to illustrate them. Here they are, all twelve of them:

Figure 1

The pentominoes

If you can find any other way to put five squares together that isn't a rotation or reflection of one of the shapes shown, then you will earn a place in history alongside Pythagoras, Newton and Professor Rubik.

In addition to the pieces, you will need a board – one of 8 × 8 cells, like a draughtsboard. It can be chequered or unchequered, but here's the important bit: each board square must be the same size as the notional squares that make up the pentominoes; or put another way, each pentomino should cover exactly five squares of the board.

Now you are ready to play though you'll need an opponent. Place the empty board between you and the pentominoes at random to one side. You take it in turns to move. A move consists of picking up one of the pentominoes from the pool and placing it on the board so as to cover five squares precisely. You may turn the pieces round or over if you wish. The winner is the last player to put a pentomino on the board. That means that the other player cannot place any of the unused pentominoes on the board without overlapping a piece that is already there.

To show you how a game goes, look at figure 2. Each piece has been numbered to indicate the order in which they were played. The second player has won because neither of the remaining pieces can be fitted into the vacant cells. If the second player had instead played one of these pieces into the bottom right corner on his last move, the first player would have won by fitting the L-shaped piece (no. 10) into the area top right.

It is possible to create a situation where no further piece will fit on the board after only five moves – this is shown in figure 3. At the other extreme, it is possible, though most unlikely, that all 12 pentominoes will be fitted on the board leaving just four vacant squares.

When you are bored with Golomb's game amuse yourself by fitting all 12 pentominoes into

Figure 2

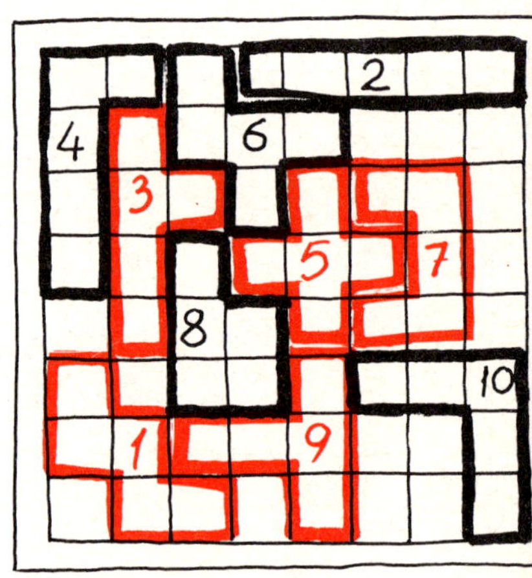

Second player wins

rectangles measuring 3 × 20 (difficult), 4 × 15, 5 × 12 and 6 × 10 (easy).

Hint

If you are first player, you will want the game to end with an odd number of pentominoes on the board, an even number if you are second player. When the board is filling up, try to estimate roughly how the remaining space can be used and plan accordingly. For example, you may, by fitting a piece in tightly, get two pieces into an area which would only take one if you played it in the centre.

Figure 3

No further plays are possible

2 PEOPLE

DOMINO DING DONG

You will need a set of dominoes and a piece of paper on which has been marked a 6 × 6 grid such that a domino exactly covers two squares of the grid.

The dominoes are placed at random face down between the players. Only the shapes, not the values are relevant to this game.

Players take it in turns to place a domino on the grid such that it covers two empty squares. To avoid a result being forced by 'copy-cat' strategy, the second player may not place his first domino symmetrically to his opponent's first domino. The last player to place a domino is the winner (or the loser if you like: it makes little difference). Look at the position in figure 1. Whoever is to play can arrange to place the last domino or force his opponent to do so.

The game can be made more difficult, and you might find more interesting, by playing the dominoes face up, again from a common pool, but requiring that where dominoes abut each other they must match. This would mean for example that two dominoes could never be placed side by side to form a square since under the rules this would require two identical dominoes and no two are the same in a set.

This game is demonstrated in figure 2. All the dominoes of the double-six pack not on the board are available in the pool. Whoever is to play will play last since there is room for three dominoes only: 1:0, 6:1 and 5:3. Of course, you cannot elect to pass your turn.

Another version of the game is to divide the pack between you and play to the same rules on a 7 × 7 or 8 × 8 grid. If you cannot play in this game you must pass. When no further plays are possible you count up the pips on your dominoes remaining in hand. Lowest scorer is the winner over an agreed number of games.

Figure 1

Figure 2

DICE GAME

ANY NUMBER

MEISCHEN

This is a Bavarian pub game akin to Liar Dice in which honesty is not always the best policy. For a good game, you need at least four players but more is better. Every player has five lives – use tokens or beer mats to represent these. The only other equipment required is a couple of dice and a shaker.

One player starts by shaking the dice and then turning over the shaker on the table so that the dice are concealed. He then examines them secretly and anounces the score which may or may not be the true score. If the two dice show different numbers, then their total is read in tens (represented by the higher of the two numbers) and units. Thus a throw of 3:5 would give a score of 53 although the player could announce this as any score he likes.

Doubles are announced as such; thus 1:1 is Double-1, not eleven. The highest score of all is 21 – Meischen. All possible scores in ascending order are: 31, 32, 41, 42, 43, 51, 52, 53, 54, 61, 62, 63, 64, 65, Double-1, Double-2, Double-3, Double-4, Double-5, Double-6, 21 (Meischen). A score falsely announced – e.g., 36 or 55 loses a life.

The first player having announced a score passes the dice, still on the table beneath the shaker, to the next player. The second player has two choices: he can either lift the shaker, implying that the first player was bluffing, or he can accept the score passed to him when he must shake the dice and then announce a score equal to or higher than the one passed him, whether or not he achieves it. The game continues like this, each player in turn either calling or accepting the dice. In the event of a call, whoever is wrong loses a life and collects a token from the central pool. When a player has accumulated four tokens and has only one life left, he tosses them into the centre when he is said to stink (use another word if you are in polite company).

Meischen costs *two* lives to the loser. Thus if you are faced with a call of Meischen, you can challenge it and risk losing two lives or you can surrender a life and start another round. The third alternative is not very attractive. You can accept the dice and roll them but you then must of course also call Meischen (as you can never call a *lower* score than the previous player). Your chances of getting a Meischen are pretty poor and you are therefore certain to be challenged when you will be collecting a couple of tokens.

The German word for challenging a score is simply 'Hoch', meaning 'Up'; in other words, lift up the shaker and let us look at the dice. The player who loses a life starts the next round.

Here is a sample round with four players, A, B, C and D.

A (rolls 2:4) '42'

B (accepts and rolls 6:4) '64'

C (accepts and rolls 1:3) 'Double-2'

D (accepts and rolls 6:2) 'Double-4'

A 'Hoch'

D loses a life.

2 PEOPLE

GO-MOKU

This game has appeared under many names, some commercial. It is usually played as a board game with pieces but it is just as easy to play with pencil and paper; all that is needed is squared paper. It is ideal for two although more can play. A sophisticated version of Go-moku is played in Japan under the name Renju. This development came about because between experts the advantage of the first move is decisive. Fortunately this flaw in the game doesn't affect most people as it takes some time to become an expert.

Your squared paper should have about 20 squares each way although you can start with less. Players have different-coloured pencils or use different marks.

The game starts with the grid empty. A turn consists of making your mark in any empty square. The object is to get five of your marks in a row, vertically, horizontally or diagonally. The five marks must be adjacent one to the other – typical winning lines are shown in figure 1, which should not give you much difficulty.

That is all there is to the game, but it's a great deal more than may appear at a first attempt. The game's potential, and that of its sister game Renju (which differs from Go-moku in putting restrictions on the first player), can be appreciated when you realise that magazines and books have been devoted to it. If you want to become a champion, then these publications are for you, provided that you are prepared to learn Japanese although there is the odd beginner's book in English.

Elementary tactics are essential knowledge. A line of three that can be extended to five in either direction is called an 'open three'. Unless an open three is stopped at one end, on the next play it can be extended to an open four which is clearly unstoppable. Take this idea a step further and you will see that two open threes (which can be created by a single play) are also unstoppable since one of them will be developed into an open four. Figure 2 shows these simple formations.

Figure 3 shows a short game in which Black, who started, is threatening an immediate five and an open four. Red is helpless. He should have played his move 8 at the other end of the open three, splitting the Black position.

Figure 1

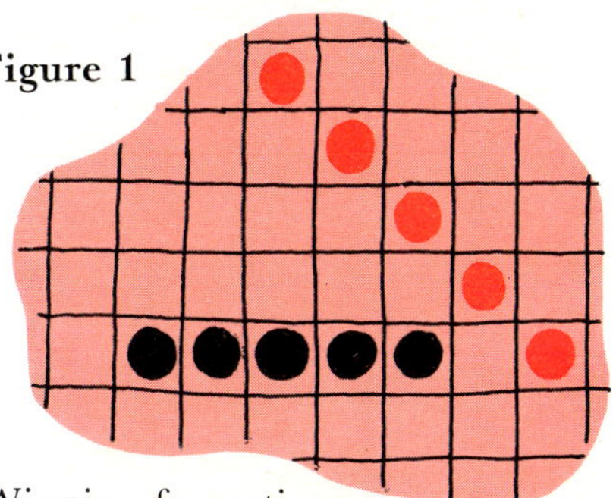

Winning formations

Figure 2

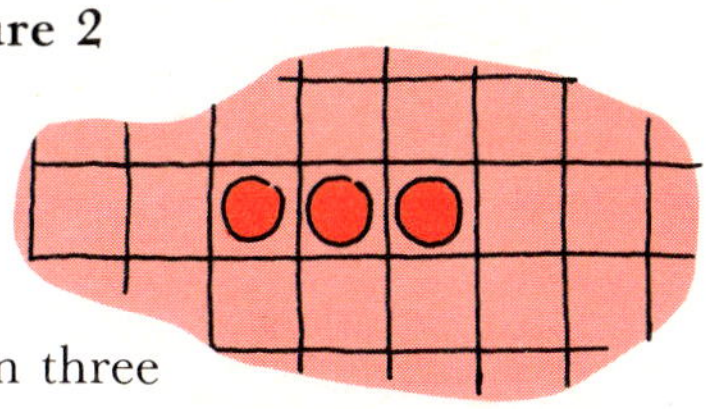

Open three

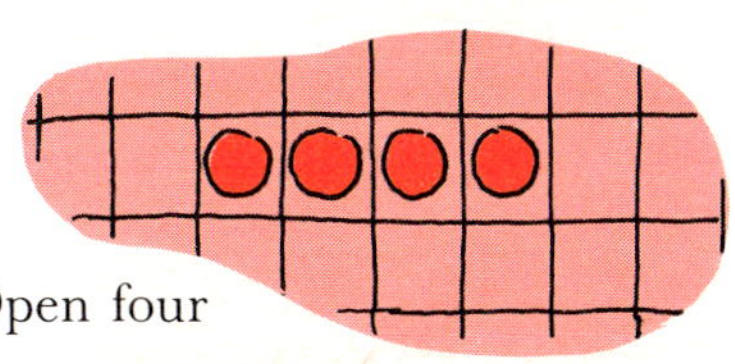

Open four

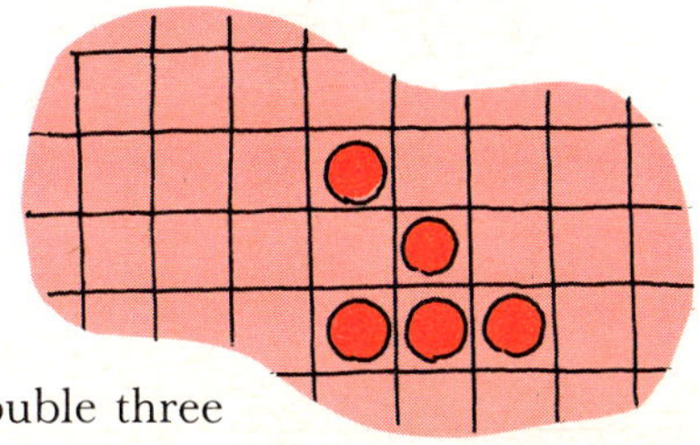

Double three

Hint

Try and keep your plays close together. Notice in the game above how all Black's plays are linked. This is hard to achieve when you are playing second but even so you should not lose sight of the aim.

Figure 3

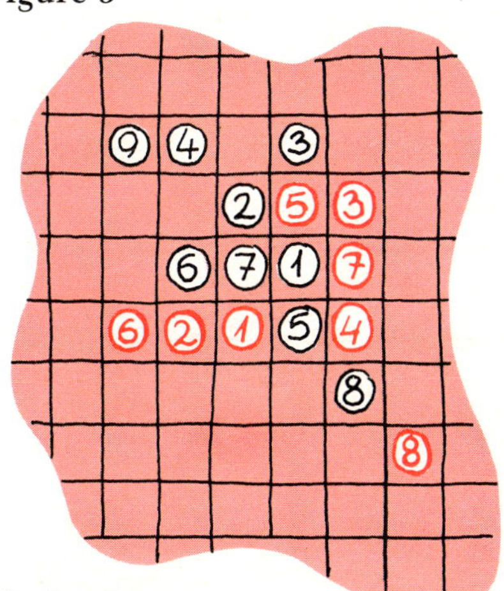

Black wins

BOARD GAME

2 PEOPLE

ARCHIMEDES

If you find Blitz Halma a bit too basic, you could try Archimedes, a game you've never heard of, which uses the same board and starting position as Blitz Halma (above) except that the men, instead of being draughtsmen, are Reversi men.

If you play Reversi or Othello (and sales figures show that millions do), you will know that these are like draughtsmen except that they are white on one side and black, or some other contrasting colour, on the other. The idea is that men can be made to change sides simply by turning them over. If you don't have a Reversi set, substitute a bit of imagination: draughtsmen can be exchanged in a central pool for example, or be suitably marked, or coins (heads and tails) can be used.

All men move like a queen in chess; that is to say any distance along a straight line, vertically, horizontally or diagonally. The move must be to a vacant square and pieces cannot be jumped, so for example the three men in the corners on each side cannot move in the starting position.

Captures are made in a unique way. Opposing men that face each other on a line, with or without vacant squares between them, are said to check each other. When a man is in check from AT LEAST THREE of the enemy, he is vulnerable to capture. A captured man is removed from the board by the capturing player, reversed to show that he has changed sides, and is then placed in the player's reserve base (which is a corner of the table in front of him) until needed. The object of the game is to capture the entire opposition.

(1) Any or all vulnerable men are captured. This is done simply by lifting them off the board, turning them over, and placing them in the reserve base. It will be seen that situations can arise where a man does not become vulnerable until another man is captured. In figure 1, the black man on the left is vulnerable, and when he is captured the second black man is vulnerable and can be taken on the same turn.
(2) The player now *either* makes a move with one of his men he has on the board *or* he introduces a man from his reserve base by placing it on any vacant square.
(3) Lastly, stage one is repeated.

Archimedes is one of those games that one could write a lot about but you will discover some of the tactics quickly enough.

And why 'Archimedes'? The inventor, Scott Marley, reminds you that the gentleman concerned brought about the destruction of a Roman fleet (or so the legend goes) by using polished shields to focus the sun's rays in the enemy's eyes, which roughly parallels the principle of capturing in the game.

Hint

Don't horde your reserves. Stop your opponent using his by forcing him to move on the board to prevent capture.

Figure 1

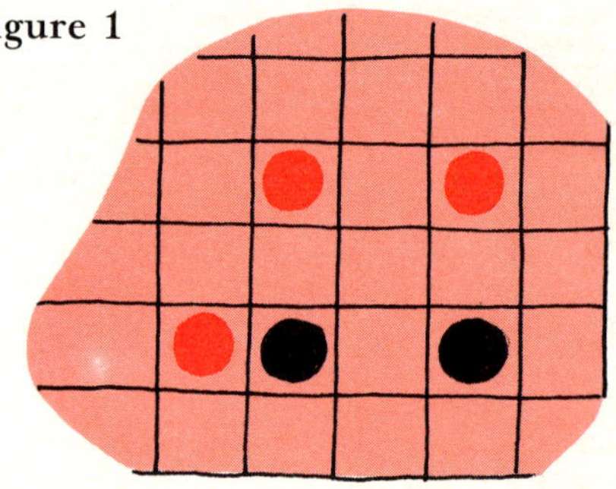

The two black men are vulnerable

2 PEOPLE

RACE GAME

ZIP

A race game of scholarly origin betrayed by the fact that it requires graph paper. Actually, any squared paper will do provided the squares are not too big or the sheet of paper is sufficiently large.

Start by drawing a race track on the paper. This should be irregular but averaging about three or four squares in width. The greater the irregularity, the more exciting the race though, of course, that may prove an overstatement.

Now join the two sides of the track somewhere by a line that follows the line of the printed grid. This is the start and finish line and the object of the game is to be the first to complete the circuit.

Place two crosses side by side, but separated by at least a square, on any two intersections of the grid on the start line. You can imagine these are Formula I cars, motor-bikes, horses, dogs, tortoises or anything else. If you lack the imagination to do this, it will not affect the game.

You take it in turns to advance your mark round the track. The rules governing movement are fairly simple. You begin by moving your mark one square. Subsequently you advance either the same distance, one square more or one square less than your previous move; in other words, you cannot accelerate or brake too sharply. If the move is along a line of the grid, the distance travelled is equal to the number of squares; if you move diagonally, the distance travelled is the number of squares on the longer side of the rectangle so formed. You cannot move to an intersection occupied by your opponent and you may not touch the edge of the circuit. Moves are illustrated in figure 1 and a completed game is shown in figure 2.

Hint

Obviously you will want to build up speed and go round as fast as possible but too fast is disastrous: to avoid leaving the circuit you will be obliged to go backwards! Plan ahead to achieve the right speeds round the bends.

Figure 1

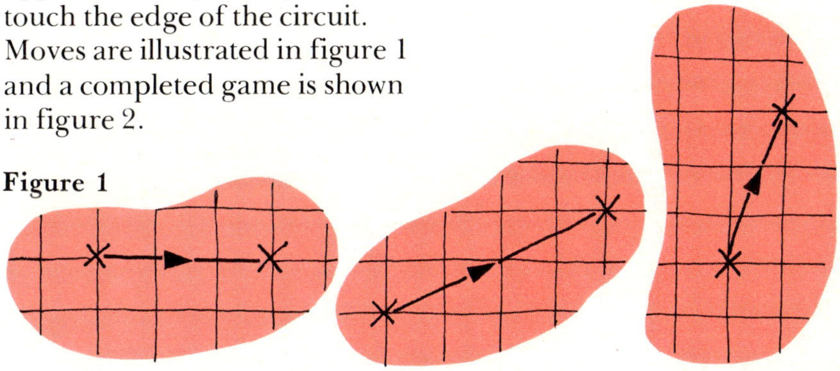

3 squares 4 squares 3 squares

Distance measurement

Figure 2

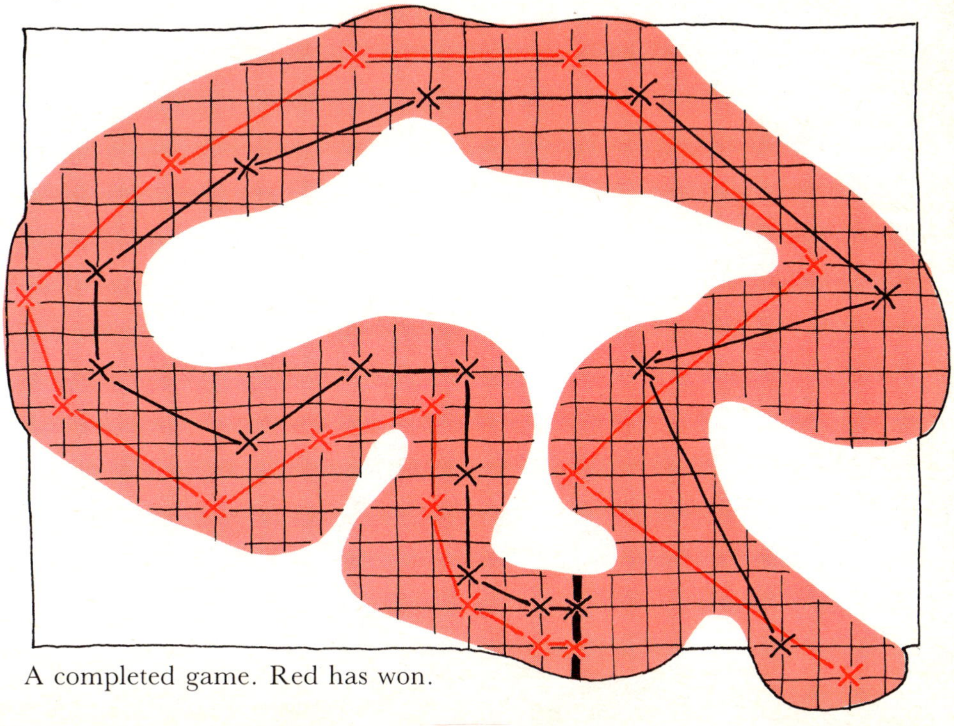

A completed game. Red has won.

BOARD GAME

2 PEOPLE

DODGEM

This looks an easy game in which the first player appears to have a large advantage – but is either impression true? Play it and decide for yourself.

First draw a 4 × 4 grid. Each player has three men in contrasting colours which are placed initially as shown in figure 1. The object of Dodgem is to get your men over to the opposite side of the board and then to bear them off, the first player to get all his men off being the winner.

A turn consists of moving a man one square straight forward or sideways but never diagonally or backwards. There is no capturing and if you can't move, that's your bad luck – you lose a turn. Once in a game each player may, on his turn and instead of a normal move, interchange the positions of one man of each colour.

In figure 1, Black is moving to the right and off the right-hand side of the board while Red is moving up the board and off the top. A game sequence is shown in figures 2 – 6. Each diagram shows one move by each side. In figure 2, Red starts by interchanging two men when Black moves. In figure 6, Red bears a man off and Black interchanges to establish a winning position since he will bear off his remaining men in four moves while Red will take five. There is rarely more than one move difference in a game.

If the first player bears all his men off and the second player bears his last man off on the very next move, the game can be adjudged a draw as each side will then have had an equal number of moves – but decide on this ruling before you start play.

You can of course increase the board in size and add more men to make the game a little more difficult (and a little longer to play) but a smaller board (3 × 3) gives a trivial contest.

Figure 1

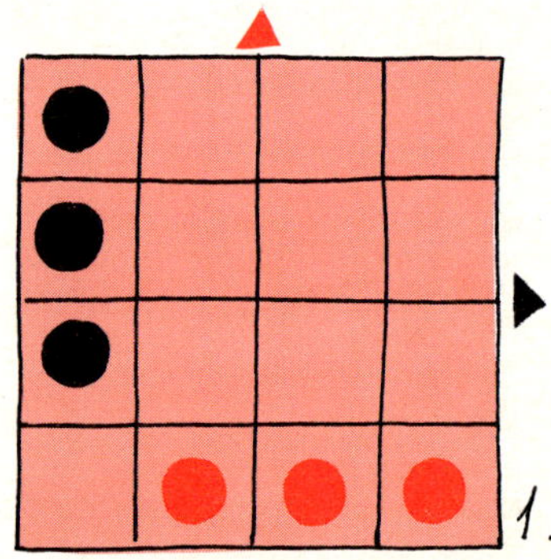

Initial position

Figures 2-6
A complete game

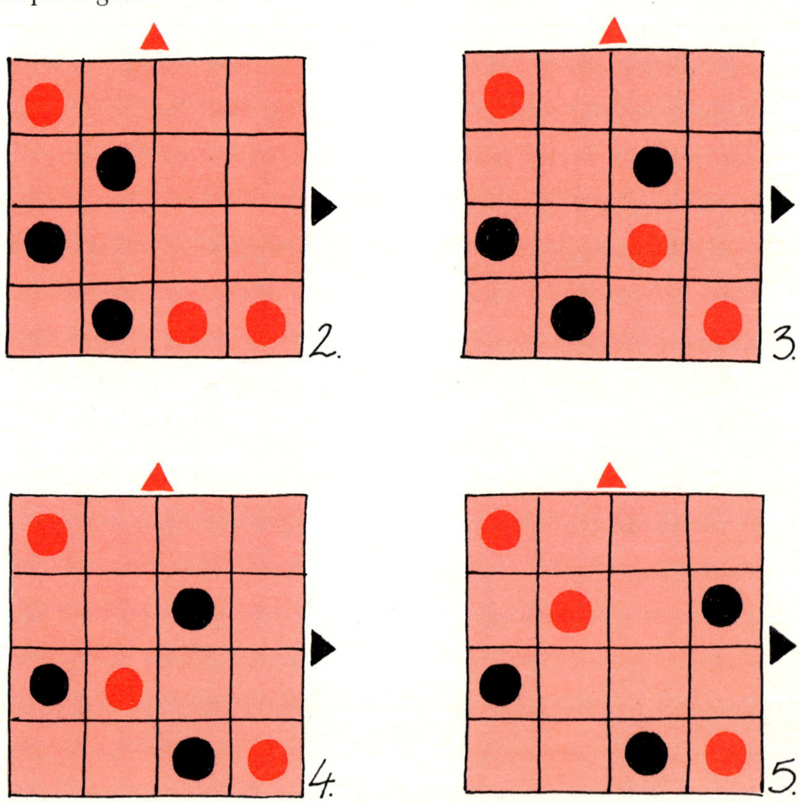

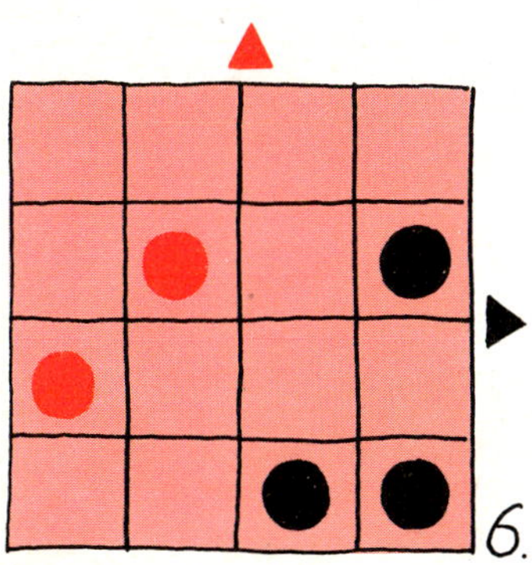

6.

WORD GAME

ANY NUMBER

HANGMAN

No book of Five-Minute Games would be complete without Hangman, an over-worked game in rather poor taste.

One player thinks of a word and then writes down a sequence of dashes equal in number to the letters in the word. A five-letter or six-letter word is the ideal.

The other players (if more than two are playing) call out a letter of the alphabet in turn with the object of discovering the hidden word. Each time a letter that is in the word is called it is entered over the appropriate dash: if it appears more than once in the word it is entered wherever it appears. If a letter is called that is not in the word then one part of the hanging man is drawn, starting with the gallows and ending usually with the man's legs, 11 items in all. If the word is discovered before the drawing is complete, the guessers have won; if not, the setter has won. Instead of nominating a letter, the word can be guessed. If the guess is wrong, then another line is added to the drawing, just as though a wrong letter had been called. A completed game is illustrated in figure 1: the guessers are triumphant.

The game can be made harder by reducing the detail of the drawing – for example, leaving out the support arm for the gallows; or it can be made easier by adding to the drawing, for example by adding two supporting legs to the gallows or including more detail on the man.

Hint

Call the vowels first: the word is certain to have one. Don't guess unless you are fairly sure that you are right.

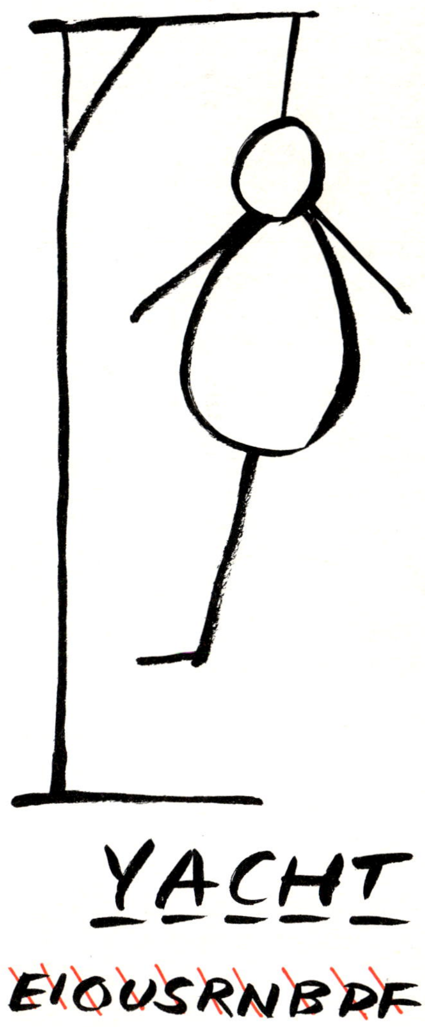

A completed game

DIAGARES

This is another of those Noughts and Crosses games, but with unusual objectives. Draw a grid of any convenient size – say, 6 × 6. One player is the attacker who uses X's (or any other symbol) while the defender uses O's or other contrasting symbol.

Players take it in turns to mark one empty square of the grid. The attacker may only mark a square which has at least one adjacent diagonal square that is either vacant or with his own symbol in it. Put another way, the attacker may not occupy a square whose adjacent diagonal squares have all been occupied by the defender.

The aim of the attacker is to make as high a score as possible by linking his symbols diagonally. Each pair of linked symbols counts 1 point. A symbol may be counted in more than one pair – for example, a line of three would score 2 points because the central symbol makes a pair with each of the other symbols. Some possible combinations with their scoring values are shown in figure 1.

The defender also scores, but in a different way. He gets 1 point for each blank square in the grid at the end of play; that is, when the attacker is unable to play because the diagonal squares adjacent to blank squares are held by the defender. This may occur after a play by either side. Naturally, the defender is not going to fill in squares gratuitously since that would deprive him of points: as soon as the attacker lacks a move the defender stops also.

Figure 1

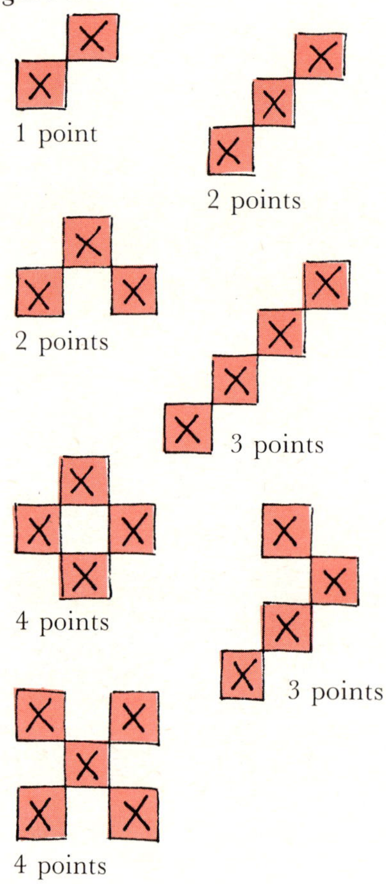

Some scoring formations

At the end of a game, points are tallied and players then change sides. A match is of two games (or any even number), the winner being the player with the higher score on aggregate.

Figure 2 shows a completed game. The defender has fared badly: he has only 4 points against his adversary's 12 points but of course there is still the other half of the match to come.

Hint

The defender has conflicting aims: stopping the attacker scoring heavily by blocking as far as possible the formation of diagonal pairs, and securing blank squares. The attacker should concentrate on the centre of the grid where it is easier to create multiple threats.

Figure 2

	O		X		O
X	O	X	O	X	O
	X	X	O	X	X
O	O	O	X	O	X
O	X	X	O	X	X
O	O	X	O	O	X

A completed game

PENCIL AND PAPER

2 PEOPLE

CIPHER CHASE

Both players draw two 6 × 6 grids. In one grid, each player enters secretly the numbers 0 – 35, one number per square, such that consecutive numbers are in adjacent squares, vertically, horizontally or diagonally. Both grids are now marked with an agreed notation so that a square can be referred to easily. An example of what one player's paper may look like at this stage is shown in the illustration. A little care is necessary in entering the numbers because if you enter them without thought it is possible to find that the grid cannot be completed because of the rule that consecutive numbers must be in adjacent squares. It may help you to draw a continuous line through the squares to start with, correcting it as necessary, before you enter the numbers. You will find that a regular arrangement is not a good idea because you want to make it difficult for your opponent to find your zero.

One player now calls out a grid reference (say, 'D4') and BOTH players announce the numbers they have in that square. The player who called out the grid reference scores the difference between the two numbers.

The second player now names a grid reference and scores in the same way, and so on. Players plot their opponent's numbers in the blank grid as they are called out. When one player calls out the grid reference of the square in which his opponent has his zero, the caller scores in the usual way but thereafter only the player whose zero was found calls out grid references, carrying on his scores until the opponent's zero is found when he scores the play in the usual way and the game ends. The player with the lowest score is the winner. Points can be counted up at the end but it is simplest to keep progressive scores.

Figure 1

6	8	9	3	4	31	32
5	10	7	5	2	33	30
4	11	6	1	34	29	27
3	12	0	35	18	26	28
2	15	13	17	22	19	25
1	14	16	21	20	23	24
	a	b	c	d	e	f

6						
5						
4						
3						
2						
1						
	a	b	c	d	e	f

Ready to start

Hint

There is a lot of luck in the game but there is some skill in both hiding your zero and, more obviously, in locating your opponent's zero.

When you have entered a few of your opponent's numbers in the blank grid, try to deduce the sequence of squares which the numbers follow, and so trace back to the zero. If you suspect the zero is in a certain area, which should therefore contain low numbers, call out those references in which your numbers are the lowest in order to keep your score down.

SOLITAIRE

If you are one of the uncounted millions who, at some time or another, have attempted to solve a Solitaire game, then the chances are that you started with the centre hole empty and attempted to reduce the position to a single marble in that hole. The chances are too that you didn't succeed. In that event, you'll be wondering why this complex and time-consuming pastime has found its way into a book supposedly devoted to five-minute games.

So here comes enlightenment. Solitaire is neither complex nor time-consuming. When you know the tricks it is a fast and fascinating game that can be played alone or in competition with others. And you don't need to go and buy a board. Just mark out a piece of card as shown in figure 1 and use counters or coins instead of marbles.

In Solitaire you start every game with one space (or hole) empty and the rest occupied. You remove a man by leaping over it, either vertically or horizontally, with an adjacent man, to an empty space immediately beyond. The two men and the empty space must be in a straight line. The man leapt is taken out of play. You are successful in Solitaire if you reduce the initial array to a single man, either on the space that was vacant at the start or in some other space.

Now back to those tricks. Figure 2 should give you some invaluable information; namely, that there are four circuits on the board and these are independent of one another – that is to say, a man can never move from one circuit to another one. On one circuit you will see that 12 jumps are possible, on two others 8 jumps and on the fourth circuit only two jumps on a move. A move, if you didn't know, is one or a series of jumps by the same man – so there is another factor in a game: how many *moves* does it take you to reach a given position?

The board can be considered as made up of blocks of six spaces and lines of three. If you learn how to remove these as entities, then all you have to do is to combine them in a series and – hey presto, you've emptied the board in no time.

To remove a line of three you need an adjacent man to act as trigger – the line can hardly remove itself! So here's how to eliminate a line of three and leave the trigger where it started (figure 3). Play a1–a3 (remove a2); c2–a2 (remove b2) and a3–a1 (remove a2). Easy isn't it?

Now for the block of six, and again we need a trigger which we want back on its starting space (see figure 4 – the trigger can also begin on other spaces: it doesn't have to be on a2 – it could also be on b2 or c2). Play a3–a1; c3–a3; a4–a2; c4–a4; a1–a3 and a4–a2.

Hint
More a word of warning than a hint: there are some combinations of starting and finishing spaces that cannot be resolved. However, you can begin with ANY space vacant and finish with a man in that space. That should be more than enough to keep you busy until it's time to try the next game.

Figure 1

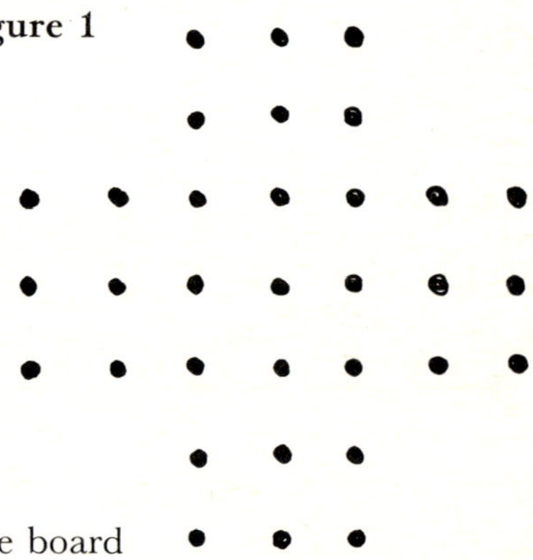

The board

Figure 2

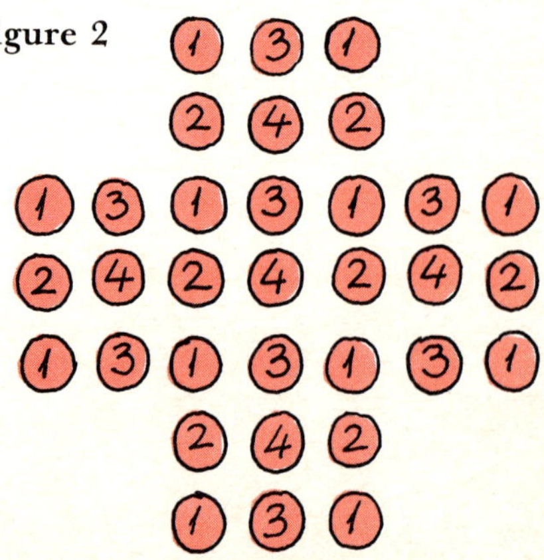

The four circuits

Figure 3

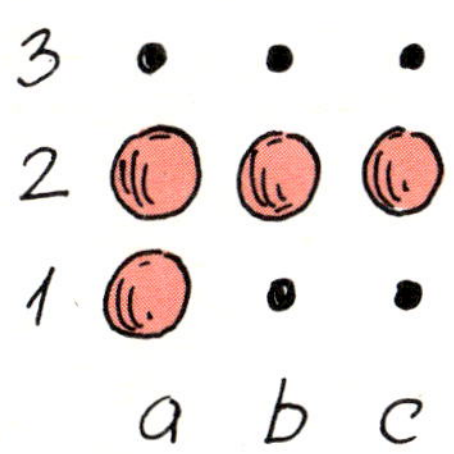

Removing a line of three

Figure 4

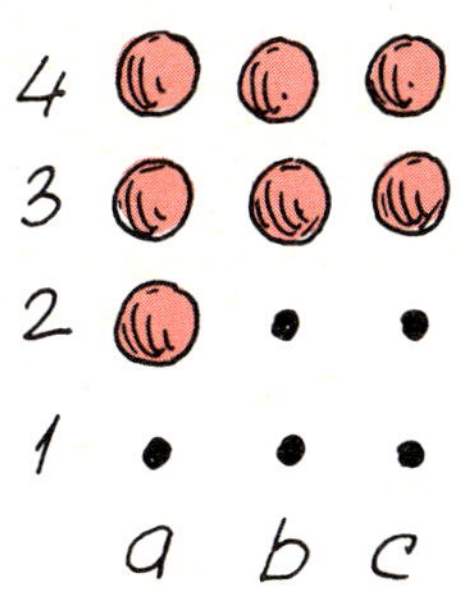

Removing a block of six

2 PEOPLE

CALCULATOR GAME

CANDLES

This game is supposed to be played with a line of 36 lighted candles. Each player in turn blows out not less than one and not more than six candles and the aim is to get your adversary to extinguish the last candle. If the idea of assembling and lighting all those candles gets on your wick, you can use a pocket calculator.

Start by entering the number 36. Both players in turn subtract any number between 1 and 6 from the total on the caculator display. The player whose turn it is when the calculator total is 1 is the loser.

Hint

If you didn't recognize it, this is one of the Nim family dressed up. That means that the winner is predestined provided he plays correctly. If you are a mathematician or are familiar with the problem, then the winner, as you will know, is you-know-who. If not, then we'll give you a hint: don't be in a hurry to start.

Even if you aren't a mathematician you will probably realise that it is a poor thing to be passed the calculator when there is just 8 remaining. Whatever you do now, you will be left next turn with 1.

2 TO 4 PEOPLE

PAY OUT

This game was developed from an idea of Phil Orbanes. First draw up a 6 × 6 grid and mark the rows and columns 1 to 6 outside the grid, as shown in figure 1. Each cell corresponds to the roll of two dice, thus the grid covers all the possible combinations of the dice. Having said that, you will need THREE dice for this game, not two.

The object is to score the most points by occupying combinations of cells. It is convenient to use different coloured pens but initials or contrasting symbols are just as good.

Players take it in turns to roll the three dice. You then select TWO of the dice for your nominated roll. For example, you might roll 5:5:2, when you could choose between 5:5, 2:5 or 5:2. If you rolled 1:4:6 you could choose between 1:4, 4:1, 4:6, 6:4, 1:6 or 6:1. Supposing in this second example, you chose 6:1. You would then mark the cell at top left; the first number always relating to the row number, the second to the column number. Once occupied, a cell cannot be used again.

The scoring combinations are as follows:

Three cells in a line (vertical, horizontal or diagonal) – 3 points
Four in a line – 4 points
Five in a line – 5 points
Six in a line – 10 points
Four adjacent cells in a square – 4 points

All scores are cumulative; thus if you score 3 points for three-in-a-row you could then add a fourth cell and score 4 more points. If you complete a line of five by filling the middle cell last however, you would only score 5 points. If you managed to occupy a block of cells in a 3 × 3 array you could count four 2 × 2 squares for 16 points.

If you are unable to make use of your dice roll because the corresponding cells are filled, you lose your turn. Finally, if you throw a triple (4:4:4 for example) you may occupy ANY cell of your choice.

A game in progress is shown in figure 2. Red leads by 16–6.

The game ends when all 36 squares are filled though it can be abandoned earlier if it is clear that neither player can add to his score.

An alternative version allows a player who cannot move on his turn to put a cross in any vacant cell to indicate that its use is denied to BOTH players.

Hint
The four central cells are the most valuable since they can be expanded in all directions. For this reason, the 3:3 and 4:4 cells should be occupied at the first opportunity as these combinations are less frequent than 3:4/4:3 which offer a choice.

Do not overlook the opportunity of blocking your opponent – the move may be more profitable than making a line yourself; for example, Red 2:5 in the above game.

Figure 1

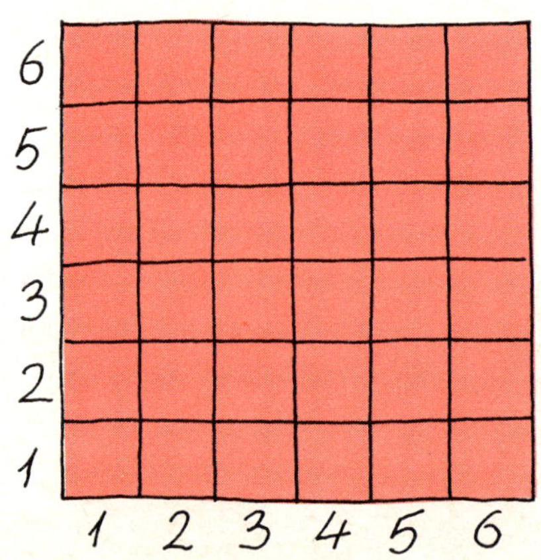

Playing area

Figure 2

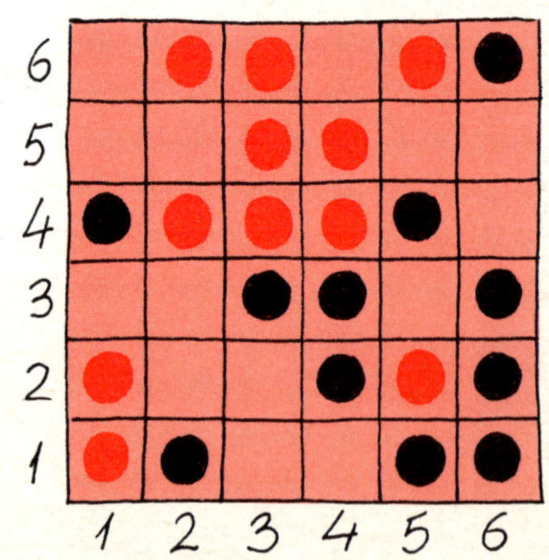

A game in progress

2 TO 6 PEOPLE

TOEPEN

This is a very popular Dutch game. It is customary to keep the score on beer mats but you might find it easier to use chips or coins. Everyone starts with 15 chips. Toepen is best for four or five players.

An ordinary pack is used from which the 2s–6s have been removed (cardplayers will recognize this as a Piquet pack). Cards rank from Ace down to 7 (in fact, they don't but since this in no way affects the game it is simpler to keep them in traditional sequence).

Toepen is a straightforward trick-taking game in the Whist tradition, but with a few twists that give it its unique character.

Four cards are dealt singly to each player. Beforehand, everyone has contributed a chip to the pool.

Now anyone may claim a new hand on the grounds that the one dealt to them does not contain an Ace or a court card. One does not have to be truthful, but one can be challenged. If challenged, whoever is wrong must contribute a further chip to the pool.

Player to left of dealer starts by leading any card from hand. Players must follow suit if possible, otherwise they must discard – there are no trumps. The winner of the trick leads to the next. However, it is only the *last* trick that counts – whoever wins it wins the hand.

At the start of play each player has only one chip at risk but at any time during the play a player may 'knock', a right executed, reasonably enough, by knocking on the table. When a player knocks, everyone, including the player who knocked, must contribute a further chip to the pool if they wish to continue playing. Any player who decides to drop out loses only his previous stake.

No player may knock twice in succession, otherwise there are no restrictions on who knocks and when. If, on a knock, a player has no chips left he may, nonetheless continue to play in that hand, but any player with chips is obliged to pay if he wishes to stay in.

At the end of a hand, the winner takes back the chips he bet but all others are left in the pool. (You may find it simpler for every player to keep the chips he bets in front of him during the game. When the game ends, all the losers push their chips into the middle.) The winner is the player who is last to have one or more chips still in hand.

An alternative method is for the winner to take the pool after each hand, but then play should be over an agreed number of hands.

Cards are not played into the centre of the table, as in Whist. Each player turns over his own cards in front of him as they are played, allowing them to overlap but with all the cards clearly visible so that before the last trick is played the three previous tricks can be examined by all the players.

There is one further rule. If a player or players start a hand with only one chip left, then all the other players must contribute TWO chips, not one.

As you see, a fast game to play with a hand taking only a minute or two – but in Toepen skill and bluff greatly outweigh chance.

Hint

If a player calls for a fresh hand, it may pay you to challenge to find out what has been discarded. It may pay you too to call for a fresh hand if, for example, you have Jack and three pip cards all in different suits, in the hope that you won't be challenged. If you are challenged, you have lost only one chip but probably have a much better hand (which you are allowed to keep).

Depending of course on the number playing, the second card in a suit may be enough to win the fourth trick but you would be lucky to get it with a single Ace – unless of course you win the third trick! You will need to play the game a bit before you can appreciate its subtleties and a lot more before you can hope to become a good player.

BOARD GAME

2 PEOPLE

NEUTRON

Neutron is an abstract game that attracted a lot of interest when introduced to a select circle of enthusiasts by its inventor, Robert A. Kraus, a few years ago.

Play is on a 5 × 5 board with each player having five men in a distinguishing colour together with one neutral piece – the neutron. The starting position is illustrated in figure 1.

All men, including the neutron, move in the same way: in any direction orthogonally or diagonally over vacant squares BUT movement must always be to the limit (last vacant square on the line). Only one man is allowed on any one square, there is no jumping and no capturing.

White plays first and moves any one of his men. The neutron is not moved. Thereafter Black and White play alternately. A turn is in two parts; first, a move with the neutron then a move with a man of one's own colour – never in the reverse order.

The object of the game is either to move, or to force the opponent to move, the neutron to a square on one's own first row – row 1 in the case of White, row 5 in the case of Black, or to reach a position where the opponent on his turn either cannot move one of his men or the neutron. If you achieve one of these, you've won.

Some idea of the strategy can be gleaned from the game position in figure 2. White to play moves Na3, e1/b4; Black replies Nb2, a5/a1 (best) when White has Ne2, c1/d2 and now Black on his next turn must move the neutron onto White's first row.

Here, to get you interested, are a couple of games. The first one shows a beginner's error: W. c1/e3; B. Nb4, c5/c1; W. Ne4, d1/d4; B. Nc2, c1/d1; W. Nc1 wins (see figure 3).

The second one finishes with an unusual win: by blocking the neutron: W. e1/d2; B. Nc4, b5/b2; W. Ne4, b1/d3; B. Na4, e5/c3; W. Nc2, a1/a4; B. Nb3, c3/c2; W. Na2, a4/a3; B. Nc4, b2/a1; W. Na2, d3/b3; B. Nb2, c2/b1; W. Na2, d2/b2 wins. (See figure 4.) Don't assume from these examples that White always wins – he doesn't!

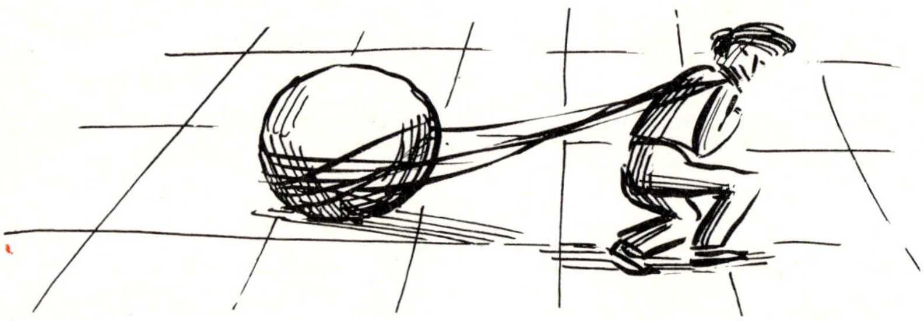

Figure 1

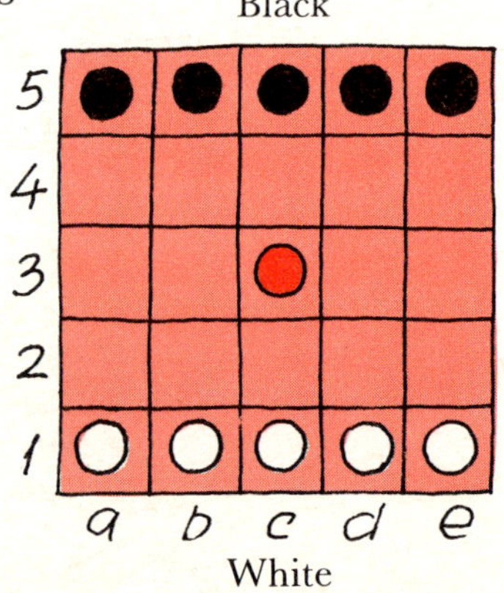

Figure 2

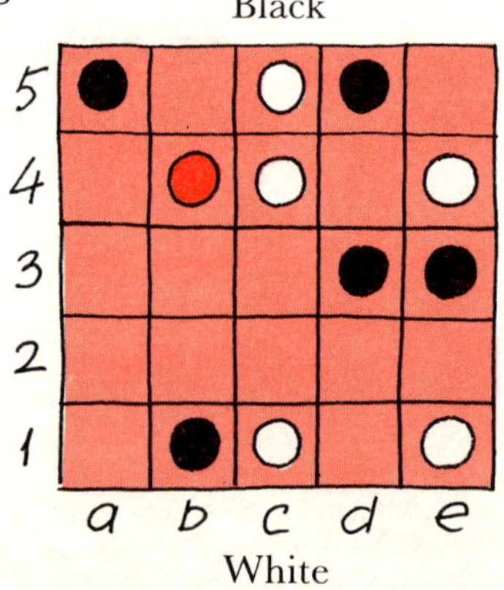

Figure 3

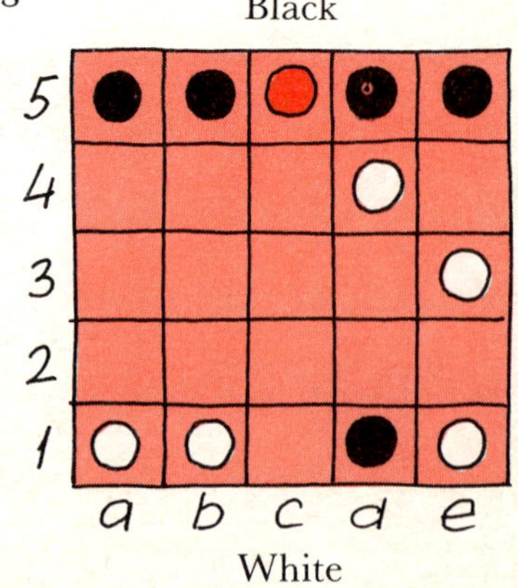

Hint

Restrict the neutron's movement with the aim of putting your opponent in a position where he will either have to move the neutron to your first row or to move it to a square where it has a free path to your first row and he is unable to block it with the move of a man so that you will be able to move it there the following turn. Figure 5 shows an example of this. It is Black to play but he has no safe square for the neutron.

Figure 4

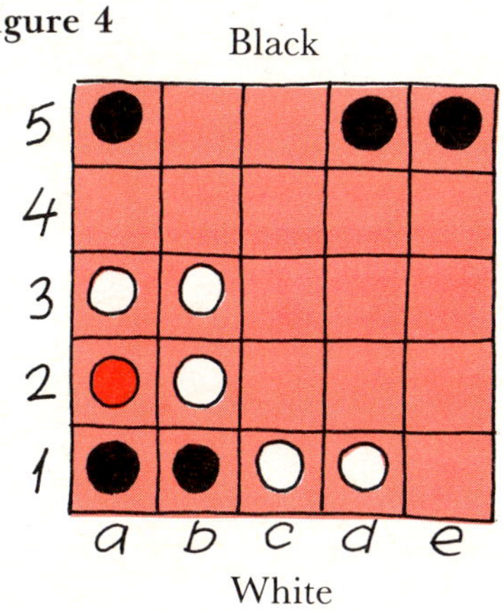

Figure 5

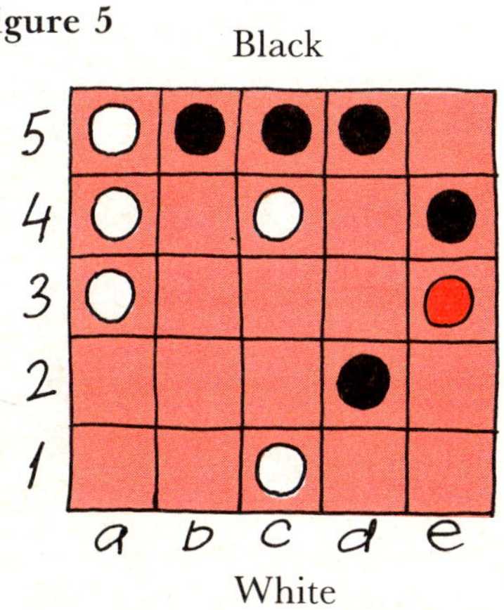

WORD GAME

SEVERAL PEOPLE

BOTTICELLI

Nothing original about this verbal game but it still may be new to you. Good post-prandial amusement if you are in intelligent company.

Someone thinks of a famous person either living or dead, or a character out of fiction, and announces his or her initial letter. Thus if Julius Caesar was in mind, the player would announce 'C'.

The other players try to discover who it is by asking indirect questions to which the quizzer must furnish the correct answer. For example, the quizzer alights on Pasternak and announces 'P'.

Q. Are you a Polish pianist?
A. No, I'm not Paderewski
Q. Are you a social reformer?
A. No, I'm not Thomas Paine
Q. Are you one of Henry VIII's wives?
A. No, I'm not Catherine Parr.

. . . and so on. If you are in familiar company, you can allow the questions to be a bit less formal:

Q. Were you a member of aircrew in Roman times?
A. No, I'm not Pontius Pilate
Q. Did you put the squaw on the hippopotamus?
A. No, I'm not Pythagoras

If the quizzer fails to give the correct response to a question then the questioner is allowed to ask him a direct question to which the quizzer must reply Yes or No. Example:

Q. Are you a female?
A. No

The player who guesses correctly takes the place of the quizzer in the next game. If you are short of players, ring up Mensa.

DICE GAME

ANY NUMBER

COMBINATIONS

Many consider this the best of all dice games. It is played all round the world in one form or another. They play it in Provence and in Puerto Rico (where it is said to be a national vice) and no doubt in Portsmouth too. It is known under so many names that there seems no harm in coining another, particularly as it is descriptive and is the first do-it-yourself version.

You'll need five dice so you will have to raid the Snakes & Ladders box (and you may think after a game or two that they are not worth putting back). The beauty of Combinations is that with the basic idea you can structure the play as you please. It is much more fun developing your own version, infinitely adjustable, than using someone else's imagination and a rigid set of rules.

Anyway, that's up to you. Here are the basics and a few ideas to get started on.

You will need some paper to draw up a scoresheet before play. On the left-hand side, running down the page, you enter some typical dice combinations and allot points for each one. Then draw a few vertical columns depending on the number of players (play by yourself if you like) and the number of games you intend to play. The game turns will equal the number of combinations you have entered.

Each player on his turn first rolls the five dice. If a player likes his roll he enters the score against one of the combinations on the scoresheet. If not, he can throw any number of the dice again, retaining those he likes. After the second roll if he likes the combination he has, he enters it on the scoresheet; if not, he is entitled to a third roll, again retaining any dice he likes (and even rolling dice that he kept back from the first roll). After the third roll a player MUST enter a score against one or other of the combinations, even if it's a zero. Only one score may be entered against each combination and when all combinations have been scored the player with the highest total is the winner (played solo, you are trying to improve on your previous score). A typical scoresheet, with explanations, is shown in figure 1. That may sound a little confusing but in fact is very simple. Suppose you threw on your first roll the dice shown in figure 2(a). You decide to keep the 4's and roll again. Now you have the dice shown in figure 2(b). You might here decide to keep the 6's as well as the 4's and roll the 3 again, hoping for a Full House. Suppose instead you decide to keep the 6's and roll the other three dice and you get the combination shown in figure 2(c). You must now score. You could elect to total the 6's when you would enter 18 in the 6 box; or you could instead choose Three of a Kind when you

Figure 1

Combination	Me	You
1		
2		
3		
4		
5		
6		
Bonus		
3 of a kind (bonus 10)		
4 of a kind (bonus 20)		
Low straight (1-2-3-4-5 bonus 20)		
High straight (2-3-4-5-6 bonus 20)		
Full House (3 of a kind and a pair bonus 30)		
Fiver (5 of a kind bonus 50)		
Total		

would enter 34 in the appropriate box.

Combinations is a matter of judgement. While at the beginning you usually have plenty of choice in which combination to go for, as the scoresheet fills your options get less and less and the game gets more and more exciting – that is, if you are the sort of person who gets excited by dice rolls.

Figure 2

Explanation:
In the NUMBER boxes enter only qualifying dice (e.g. 6:4:4:4:1 — enter 12 in 4 box).
Enter Bonus (say 25) if total of NUMBER boxes exceeds 60.
In all other boxes enter total of ALL dice plus applicable bonus (e.g. 5:5:5:5:2 — enter 42 in 4 of a kind box).

Hint

If you are squeezed and are left with say the 2 and 6 boxes open and end up with a roll of 6:5:5:3:1, you would be advised to enter this as a zero in the 2 box rather than a six in the 6 box as you would normally hope to score more 6's than one. Fiver is also a good box for zeros since this is a very hard roll to get.

2 PEOPLE

MAYPOLES

Draw two parallel lines of evenly-spaced dots on a piece of paper. The lines should be about 5 cm apart (if you're not in to old-fashioned metric, that's about 2″). Half-a-dozen dots on each line is about right for a quick game.

You will need a biro each in contrasting colours; if these are not available, use any pen or pencil to hand and let one player draw dotted lines and the other continuous lines, because lines are what you draw – one each turn, joining a dot on one line to a dot on the other. The line must be more-or-less straight and you cannot connect two dots that have previously been connected. One other important restriction (which is what the game is really about) is that you cannot cross one of your own lines.

The object is to draw the last line – i.e., leave your opponent without a legal play. Alternatively, you can make the winner the player who *doesn't* draw the last line.

A completed game is shown in the diagram. Red is unable to play.

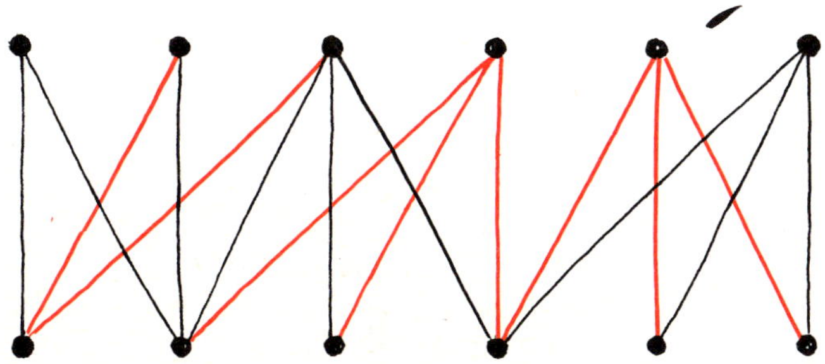

A completed game

MATCHES GAME

2 PEOPLE

NIMMCLOCK

Nim means literally to take or steal. Nim games, which are supposed to be of Chinese origin though you'd find that hard to prove, are those in which two players take it in turns to remove a number of objects (matches are popular) from one of a number of rows or heaps with the object of taking, or of not taking, as prearranged, the last object.

Nimmclock is a nim game with a difference. For a start, it comes from Australia where, as everyone knows, the clocks are upside down.

Begin by drawing a clockface and then use matchsticks to mark the hours (see figure 1). Each player in turn now removes 1, 2 or 3 matchsticks. If more than one matchstick is taken, then each must be in sequence on the clockface. For example, you could take 3, 4 and 5 in a turn but not, say, 6 & 8. The player who takes the 12 o'clock matchstick is the loser.

Now, all Nim games are predictable: that is to say, given the conditions of a game it can be determined who will win from the outset with correct play. Nimmclock is no exception. Once you know its secrets you will win consistently, to the bafflement and admiration of your friends.

As in all Nim games, there are winning positions and losing positions in Nimmclock. ALL the losing positions have an odd number of matchsticks – that is, the 12 o'clock matchstick plus an even number of others. That does not mean that all positions with an odd number of matchsticks are lost – it depends on the groupings. Here is a game with the numbers indicating which matchsticks are removed:

9, 10; 3, 4, 5; / 11; 6; / 2; 7; / and the first player loses. Now you have the idea you might care to study a few winning and losing positions (figure 2).

Hint

Actually, a lot more than a hint: a hundred-percent stone-cold certainty. Play first and take either 5, 6, 7 or just 6 – and thereafter take the corresponding match or matches to those removed by your opponent (for example, he takes 1, 2; you take 10, 11). When your opponent discovers this ploy – and not of course before – you can suggest that the first player may not take the 6 – this makes the game just a little bit harder!

Figure 1

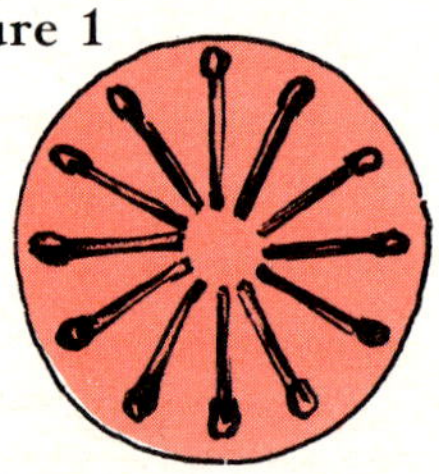

Starting position

Figure 2

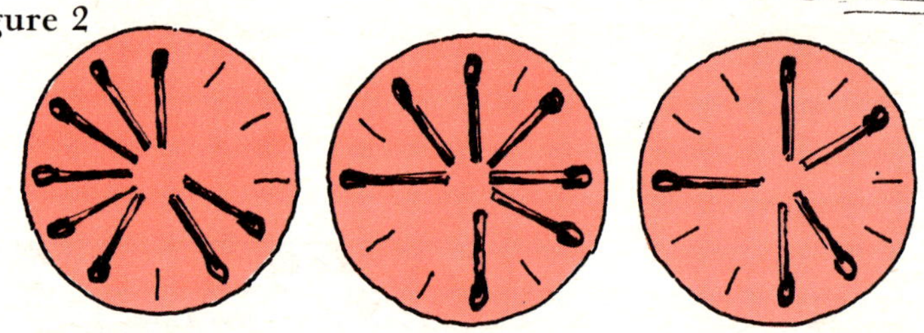

Winning positions with the move

Losing positions with the move

BOARD GAME

2 PEOPLE

NINE MENS MORRIS

Nine-men's-morris was popular in medieval times but is hardly played at all now. Many old churches have Nine-men's-morris boards scratched in pews but we recommend that you don't use these as it is quite simple to draw up your own board (as illustrated).

When you've done that, you'll need two sets of nine men, preferably in contrasting colours or appearance. Almost any small objects will do: counters, coins, tokens, bottle tops, Smarties etc.

You start by placing the empty board between you. Only the points (intersection of lines) are used. At each turn, you enter one of your men by placing it on any vacant point. The object is to get three of your men in a straight line; that is, linked by a single line of the board. As you are reading this book, you are almost certainly much too bright to allow your opponent to complete a line of three and we will assume for the moment that your opponent, though not as bright as you, does not allow you to make a line of three either.

So now the 18 men are on the board and there are six vacant points. Hereafter your play consists of moving one man to an adjacent vacant point, still with the same aim of making a line of three (or the opposite aim of stopping your opponent making one, which amounts to the same thing).

When you complete a line of three you garner your reward: the privilege of removing one of your opponent's men from the game. A line of three, since you are now ready to learn a little more about the game, is referred to by old pews-players as a mill. Some players do not allow you to remove a man from an opponent's mill.

If one player is blocked so that he cannot move, then the other player continues to play until the opponent is able to move, when players again alternate.

When the forces of one player are reduced to three men then he may move to any vacant point, not just an adjacent vacant point. When a player is reduced to two men he is the loser. Draws are not infrequent. If, when placing your men on the board initially, your opponent allows you to make a mill then you remove one of the men he has already placed, as in the second stage of the game.

A decided lead is usually necessary to force a win when the third stage is reached. If neither side possesses this and no decision is being reached – for example, in the case of four men against three men – the game should be abandoned. The player with the most men can win half a point, or you can score the difference between the numbers of men on each side and maintain a points score that runs on from one game to the next.

Figure 1

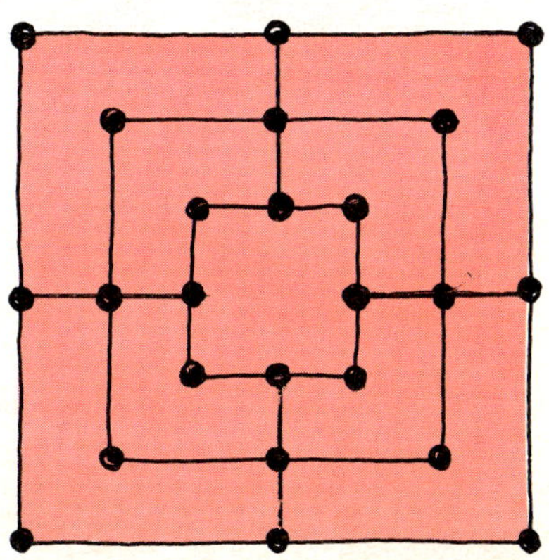

Board

Hint

There are only four opening moves to be considered: all others are reflections or orientations of these. Try to keep the initiative (which you will have if you start) so that your opponent is obliged to follow you around to block your mills thereby scattered his forces. Sooner or later the position should break in your favour. Unfortunately (or fortunately, if you happen to be the second player) what often happens is that the defender at some point makes a play that is also an attack, requiring a response when the initiative passes to him. Compare Go-moku, another game of alignment where this situation occurs. Notice that there are four points which can be considered as key points to be occupied if possible: the points that extend in four directions.

PENCIL AND PAPER

2 PEOPLE

CRYSTALS

This is a difficult game to understand but it is well worth the effort since it is quite unlike other games you've played – it offers what the copywriters might call a 'new dimension'. Crystals is also disputatious: the chances are that you should be able to get a few good arguments going on what is and what is not allowed.

Before you can play Crystals you will need some squared paper. For a quick game, use a 15 × 15 grid. It is desirable that each player has a different-coloured pen.

You take it in turns to fill in one cell of the grid, known as an atom. Your aim is to make crystals – the bigger the better, since you score 1 point for every cell in them. The game ends when players are agreed that no more crystals can be formed.

So far, simple enough. All you need to know now is what is and what is not a crystal, and that is a little more difficult. A true crystal is a wonder of nature: it has perfect symmetry around all four of its major axes – vertical, horizontal and the two diagonals – think of a Union Jack (but not too hard, because the game is not about flags).

A crystal in this game is a two-dimensional version of a true crystal; that is to say, the shape must be capable of being divided along its major axes into four pairs of mirror images. For an example look at typical crystals in figure 1.

You will be glad to know that you don't have to fill in all the squares of a crystal in order to score it; it is sufficient to have just four atoms inside it – but there must be none of your opponents' atoms within its boundaries. A crystal must be solid: it cannot have a hole in it, like a mint. The hole in this case would be the presence of a foreign atom (figure 2). Also, a crystal cannot include an atom that is joined to it by a corner (figure 3).

An example of play is given in figure 4 to show you exactly how to construct a crystal. You (red) have just played in figure 4(a) and announce a crystal. You strive to make it as big as possible remember – but it must be regular and must not contain an opponent's atom. You cannot do better than the one in 4 (b), which you outline in your colour and then announce the score – 17 points. No player, you included, can now play within the crystal. Note that in claiming it you have depleted your active strength by four atoms. This is a fair buy, but sometimes it will pay you not to claim a small crystal, earning only a few points, if some of your four atoms can contribute to the construction of a bigger crystal. The game now continues. Your opponent might, for example, play an atom within the outlined cross, and scores 9 points.

Figure 1

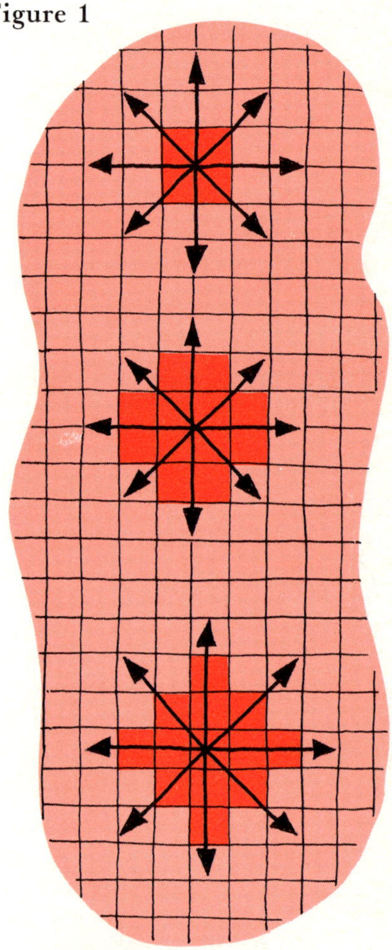

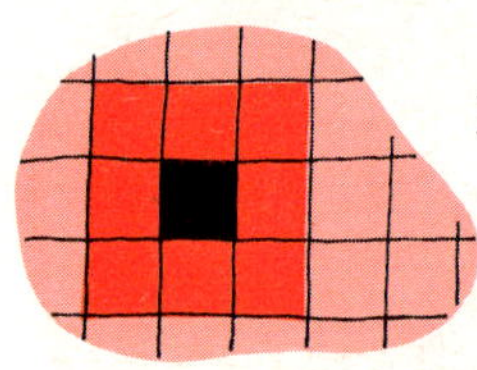

Figure 2

Figure 3

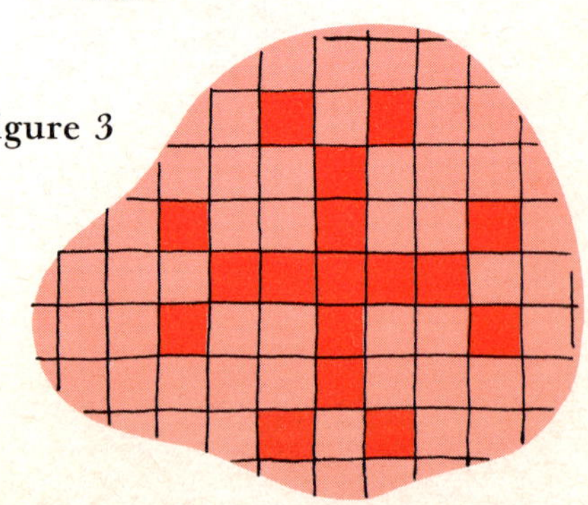

Hint

If you are second or third player, you will be advised to deploy a few atoms defensively to prevent the first player, who has a considerable advantage, forming a large crystal early in the game. Later, as the board is sprinkled with rival atoms, it will be hard for anyone to make big gains.

Figure 4a

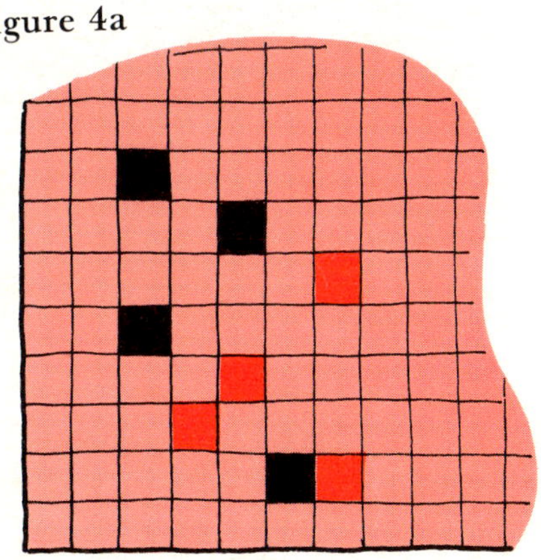

Figure 4b

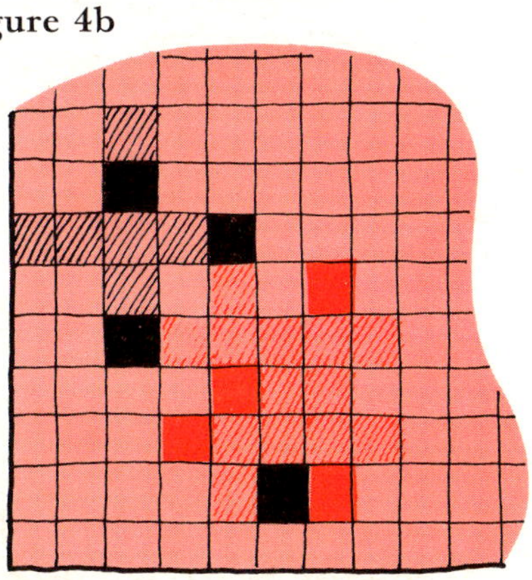

2 PEOPLE

NUMBER SQUARES

Start by drawing a 4 × 4 grid and write below it the numbers 1 to 16 inclusive.

Each player in turn enters one of the available numbers in a blank square in the grid, crossing the number off below the grid as he does so. Only numbers that have not been used are available so that if the grid is filled every number 1–16 will appear in it.

You must avoid entering a number that has a consecutive number in any adjacent square, orthogonal or diagonal. You lose if you cannot do this.

A consecutive number is a number that immediately precedes or follows the number played – e.g., 7 and 9 are consecutive numbers of 8. Two numbers, 1 and 16, have only one consecutive number each (2 and 15 respectively).

In the example in figure 1 the first player loses since he will be forced finally to play in the square at the left centre – and none of the three remaining numbers are eligible.

Figure 1

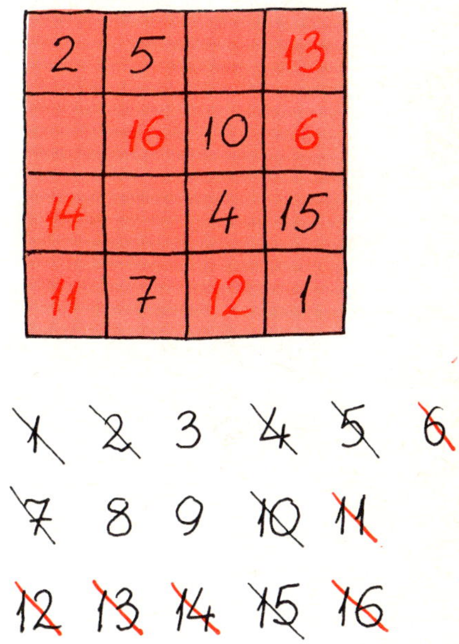

An end position

COIN GAME

2 PEOPLE

PENNY ROYAL

If you have ever wondered what to do with all those ½p's you keep getting in change, you could do worse than find an opponent and play Pennyroyal. You will need ten coins, and if that's too many, 10p pieces will do as well if you happen to be that rich – but you can't mix coins.

Arrange them heads-up at the start of the game in the form of a pyramid so that they just touch one another (figure 1). We have numbered them for reference but you would not need to do this in a game unless you were planning a post mortem.

Players take turns to move and the last to do so is the winner. A move consists of *sliding* a head-up coin from its position in the array, turning it over (that makes it tails) and sliding it back so that it *nestles* against *at least* two other coins. Notice the word nestles: you cannot slide a coin between two others though you may slide one from this position. Examples of legal and illegal nestles are shown in figure 2.

There are a few other things that you can't do:

(1) You must never move any coin in the array other than the one you are sliding out of and into position;
(2) You cannot slide a coin back into the position from which you have just removed it;
(3) You cannot leave a coin in isolation from the array;
(4) You cannot move any tail-up coin.

It follows from the last rule that ten moves is the maximum possible in this game.

In figure 3, for example – it's only part of an array – you cannot move either of the marked heads-up coins because in one case it could not be done without disturbing the array and in the other it would mean a coin is left isolated.

Here is a short game. The first number is the coin moved while the other numbers are the coins against which it is nestled.

Player A	**Player B**
1 – 6, 10	2 – 1, 3, 6
7 – 8, 9	4 – 2, 3
8 – 7, 9, 10	5 – 3, 4
10 – 3, 6, 9 wins	

The end position is shown in figure 4.

Figure 1

Starting array

Figure 2

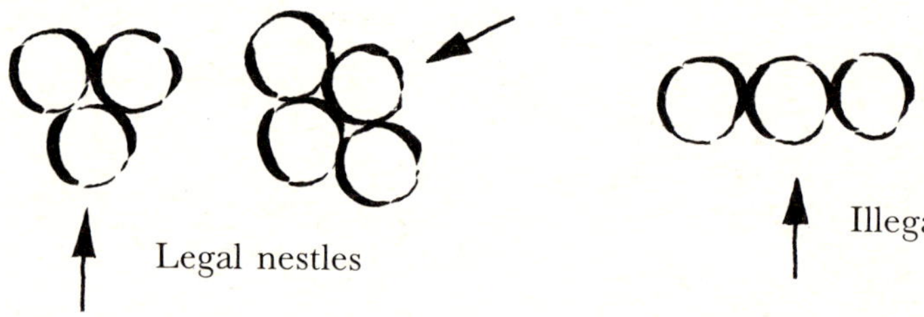

Figure 3

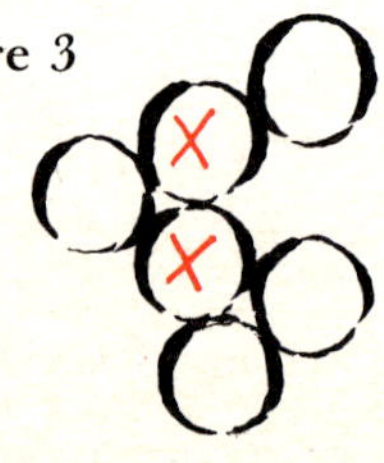

Marked coins cannot be moved

Figure 4

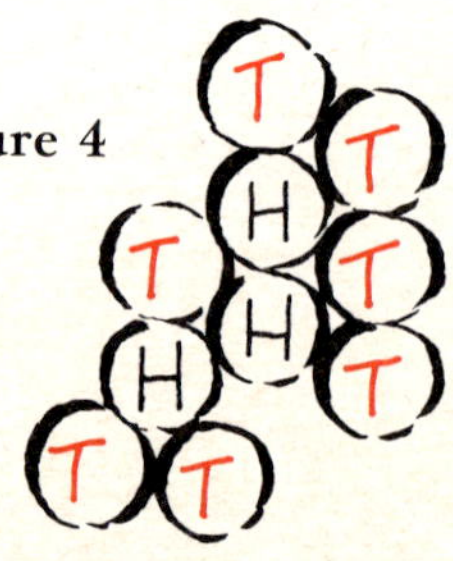

End position

DARTS

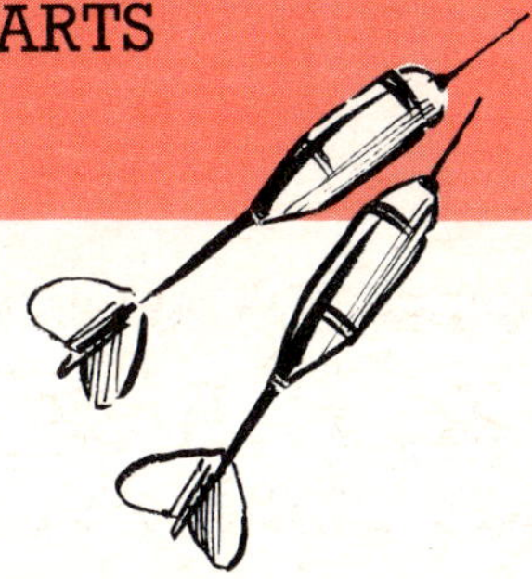

ANY NUMBER

BANG ON!

This game was invented by David Parlett. You will need a dartboard, a set of darts and a good eye, plus a blackboard or paper to score on.

First player starts by throwing his three darts to make the highest possible score – he does not have to throw a double. The second player now strives to equal, or get as close as possible above or below, the first player's score. Second player does not have to throw all his three darts: for example, if Player 1 scored 47 and Player 2 notched a double-20 followed by an eight, he has almost achieved the ideal – an equal score – and surrenders the last dart. The first player now *adds the difference* of the two scores, if any, to his original total. If more than two are playing, all in turn try to match the first player's total, the first player always scoring the difference between his original score and those of the other players. When everyone has had a turn, first player throws again and attempts to match his original total. Each of the other players score the difference between the first player's totals, if any. Notice that the first player does not score his second throw.

That ends the first round. Scoring in a four-player game might look like this:

A	B	C	D
47			
1 (B scored 48)			
17 (C scored 64)			
9 (D scored 38)			
(59)	12	12	12
74	12	12	12

Now it is the second player's turn to have a free throw, and the same procedure is followed exactly. When everyone has had a turn the game is over – unless, of course, you have all got more than five minutes to spare when there is nothing to stop you having another go, and another . . . Highest score at the end of play wins, if you didn't guess.

Hint

Naturally, you will want to score 'Bang on', but don't risk going heavily over the top in order to match a score. For example, if you were five short of the required total it would be risky aiming for the 5, with a 20 on one side and a 12 on the other, unless you are a good darts player.

2 PEOPLE

THE T-GAME

This ingenious little time-filler was invented by Christiaan Freeling who claims it is better than Edward de Bono's *L-game*, from which it is derived, because it is easier to visualise ahead.

Mark out a board as in figure 1. Each side has five men in contrasting colours, positioned initially as in figure 2. Play is on the intersections (if you prefer to play on squares, mark out a 4 × 4 board). Each side moves in turn and you cannot opt not to move. The object is to leave the opponent without a legal play.

All men move in the same way, to an adjacent intersection along a line of the board; thus diagonal movement is not allowed. There are two restrictions:

(1) It is forbidden to return with the same man to the point you left on the preceding play (so you cannot move a man to-and-fro between two points).
(2) You must always keep a line of three of your men, either vertically, horizontally or diagonally (notice that although diagonal moves are not allowed, a line of three is).

Whoever starts has a choice of four moves (see figure 2 again) which, you will note, all maintain the mandatory line of three. Draws are possible.

Here is a quick game. Red moves first.

1. c1–d1, b2–b1
2. d1–d2, c3–c2?
3. b3–c3!) c1–d1
4. b1–c1 wins

(see figure 3)

(? = bad move; ! = good move)

Hint
Try to retain maximum flexibility so that you can switch from one line of three to another: remember that there are only six free points and it is easy for one's forces to be split so that the line of three is immobilised as happened in the above game.

Figure 1

The board

Figure 2

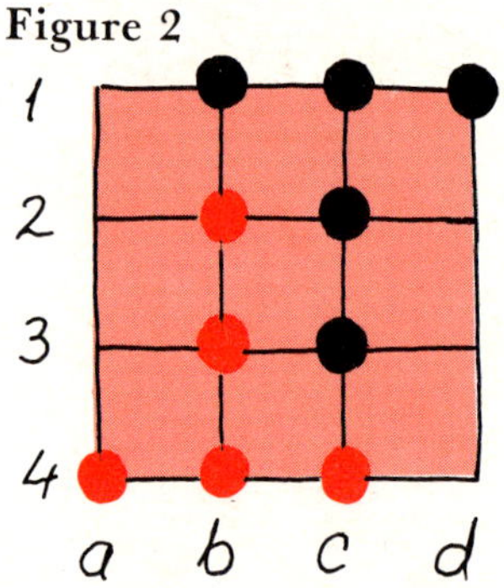

The starting position

Figure 3

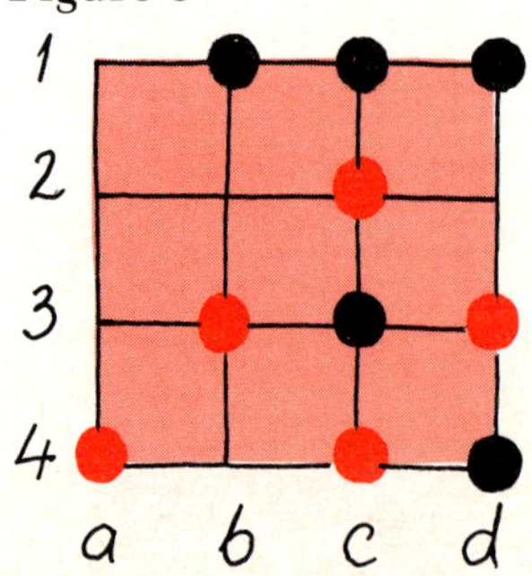

Final position

2 PEOPLE

DOUBLE POKER

You need to be familiar with Poker hands to play this game but, unlike Poker, no gambling is involved.

You want a standard pack of cards (less the jokers) and plenty of table room. Each of you maps out a notional 5 × 5 card array; that is to say, you both find enough room to put down 25 playing cards roughly in a square. Now place the pack, having shuffled it, of course, face down between you. One starts by taking the top card off the pack, turning it over and placing it anywhere within his notional square.

The second player now does likewise, and so on, turns alternating, until both squares are complete. Each player then takes one of the two remaining cards and may, but is not obliged, to change if for any card in his array, the card it replaces being removed from the game. The object is to make the best score with the ten poker hands formed by the five rows, five columns and two long diagonals. Here is how you score:

A pair (any two cards of the same rank) – 1 point
Two pairs – 3 points
Flush (five cards of the same suit) – 5 points
Three of a kind – 6 points
Full house (three of a kind and a pair) – 10 points
Straight (five cards in sequence, suits disregarded; Ace high or low) – 12 points
Four of a kind – 15 points
Royal flush (a straight in one suit) – 30 points

Cards that do not contribute to one of these combinations do not score. For example, ♡A, ♡K, ♡Q, ♣2, ◇2 in a row scores just 1 point for a pair; the high cards earn nothing.

A game array, with scores marked, is illustrated in figure 1.

Hint
Place middle-value cards (e.g., 7, 8, 9) in the centre of the array since they are the easiest to convert into the high-scoring straights.

CARDS

2 PEOPLE

CALYBRAT

This is a game that was once played a lot in Poland and maybe still is. It is clearly related to the modern game of Cassino.

You need a standard pack of cards with the jokers removed. Suits are ignored. Cards are valued according to their pip count with Ace as 1, Jack 11, Queen 12 and King 13. Four cards are dealt singly to each player and a further four cards are dealt face up to the table. The object is to capture the most cards (values ignored).

Play alternates, and on each turn one card is ALWAYS played from hand. If one or more of the table cards sum to the value of the card played, then all are gathered in by the player and kept to one side. For example, a player puts down a King and picks up an Ace, 3 and 9 (since these total 13), picking up all four cards. If a player cannot match from his hand, or doesn't want to, or there are no cards on the table, then the played card is left face up and can subsequently be matched by either player – i.e., it becomes part of the table display.

When all four cards in hand have been used – after four turns, of course – then a further four are dealt and so on, but no further cards are dealt to the table. A player can (and must) put down one card only from hand, thus a King on the table can only be matched by a King from hand.

If a player can match a table card with one of the same rank from hand (Queen and Queen for instance) he can announce 'Stick' when the two cards are frozen. Frozen cards can only be picked up by matching a second time with a card of the same rank. The point of this is if you have two cards of the same rank you can usually dispose of them by freezing whereas without this facility you are likely to be left with one in hand. When all cards have been played, the player who took the last card from the table also takes any remaining there.

The player with the most cards is the winner.

Hint

If you have a pair which you cannot match on the table, play one down and you are likely to be able to win it next turn.

CALCULATOR GAME

2 PEOPLE

SUM LINES

Do you have a pocket calculator? Nothing elaborate, just one with the four basic functions and the usual digits? That's all you need for Sum Lines together with a small piece of paper and a couple of coloured pens.

First draw a 3 × 3 magic square which includes the digits 1–9 once each – only one is possible (figure 1) though of course you can have it round different ways. Now take your calculator and enter the digits 123 in that order. This is your starting number. Now you take it in turns to enter ONE function followed by ONE digit; for example, you might enter +7 or ×4 – the four functions you can use are of course plus, minus, multiply and divide.

The object is to try and make the calculator read one of the lines in the magic square. There are eight of these: three rows, three columns and two diagonals. The number can be read forwards or backwards but the digits must be in the correct sequence. Thus 276 would be all right, but 627 wouldn't do.

When you succeed in matching a number you put a line through the three digits in the square using your colour pen. When all eight lines have been matched, the player with the higher score wins. Draws are clearly possible but you could get over this by awarding the game to the first player who gets four lines. Agree this beforehand if there is a risk of your coming to blows.

What happens when the display comes up with a four-figure number? No problem: just ignore the first digit. So if you had 647 and elected to multiply by 2, you would get 1294. Ignore the 1 and you have 294 – a line!

Here's the start of a game.

A – 123 × 3 = 369
B – 369 − 8 = 361
A – 361 − 4 = 357 (line)
B – 357 × 2 = 714
A – 714 × 3 = (2)142
B – 142 × 9 = (1)278
A – 278 − 2 = 276 (line)

So A is doing rather well (see figure 2).

Figure 1

6	7	2
1	5	9
8	3	4

Magic square

Figure 2

6	7	2
1	5	9
8	3	4

Player A in the lead

Hint

With careful play, neither side should be able to get a line. You can make the game more difficult by allowing (or requiring) two digits to be computed each time – or does it make the game easier?

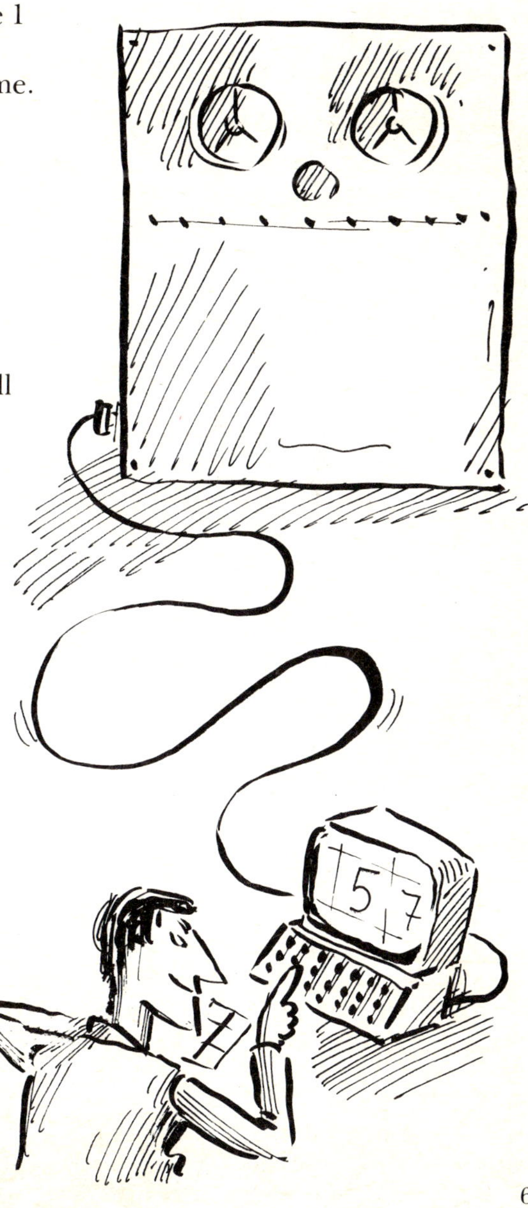

ANY NUMBER

WORD FISHING

This new and highly entertaining game was invented by Malcolm Fraser who happens to live in New Zealand where fishing of the coarse variety is something of a national sport. However, all you need for this version in an egg cup, representing the net, and an area of solid print such as you will find in a newspaper, magazine or book. Anything at all specialised like a telephone directory or croquet results is not suitable. The page is the sea and the words are your fish.

Two or more can play. You start by agreeing a quota of points – a trial run will indicate a suitable figure, but say 200. The points correspond to letters.

Each player now 'baits his hooks' by breaking down his point allocation into numbers, representing words. Numbers must be 4 and upwards, and add up to the agreed total. You are now ready to go fishing.

Each player in turn searches the print for an area in which the fish distribution looks as though it corresponds fairly closely to his bait. No more than one minute each allowed for this: you can't expect the fish to stay still, can you? Now reverse the egg cup (take the egg out first) over the selected area and draw a line round it. The catch consists of all the words in the circle. Words which are partly inside and partly outside the circle count as part of the catch as long as at least one letter is completely inside the line.

The next step is to match up the words caught inside the circle with the baited numbers. A given number will catch a word of exactly that length, or a shorter word. You cannot however combine two numbers to catch a longer word and you cannot catch two fish on one hook – you can't add two word lengths together and score both words with the one number. So you can catch a 6-letter word with number 6 or a higher number; but not with a 5 or two 5s. Number 6 would also catch a smaller word from 1 letter up to 5 letters, but only one such word. You score 1 point for each letter in all words that qualify.

The winner of course is the player with the higher or highest score.

In case you are not a fisherman, here is an example of a catch in a game in which the agreed total was 200 points. The player netted 182 – a respectable score.

Hooks	Fish
13	11
10 10	9 9
9 9 9	9 8 7
8 8 8	7 7 6
7 7 7 7	6 6 6 6
6 6 6 6 6	6 6 5 5 5
5 5 5 5 5 5	5 5 5 5 5 5
4 4 4 4 4 4	4 4 4 4 4 4 4
Total: 200	Total: 182

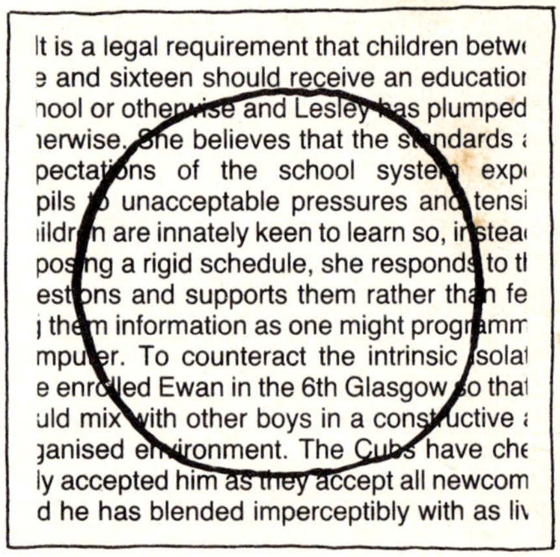
It is a legal requirement that children betw
e and sixteen should receive an educatio
hool or otherwise and Lesley has plumped
herwise. She believes that the standards a
pectations of the school system expe
pils to unacceptable pressures and tensi
ildren are innately keen to learn so, instea
posing a rigid schedule, she responds to t
estions and supports them rather than fe
g them information as one might programm
mputer. To counteract the intrinsic isola
e enrolled Ewan in the 6th Glasgow so tha
uld mix with other boys in a constructive a
ganised environment. The Cubs have che
ly accepted him as they accept all newcom
d he has blended imperceptibly with as liv

Hint

You cannot avoid losing points on words of three letters or less, so look out for an area in which there is a minimum number of short words.